T0120822

IMPERCEPTIBLE REALITY

A Longing for Spiritual Vision

CONNIE BERTELSEN YOUNG

WESTBOW
PRESS®
A DIVISION OF THOMAS NELSON
& ZONDERVAN

WestBow Press books may be ordered through
booksellers or by contacting:

WestBow Press
A Division of Thomas Nelson & Zondervan
1663 Liberty Drive
Bloomington, IN 47403
www.westbowpress.com
844-714-3454

ISBN: 978-1-6642-4905-9 (sc)
ISBN: 978-1-6642-4906-6 (e)

Print information available on the last page.

WestBow Press rev. date: 11/19/2021

So we fix our eyes

not on what is seen,

but on what is unseen,

since what is seen is temporary,

but what is unseen is eternal.

(2 Corinthians 4:18 NIV)

Books by Connie Bertelsen Young

Signs of The Time
Esprit De Corps
You're Only Old Once
Heart Words
The House of You
Imperceptible Reality

CoNteNts

Dedication

To those who know there is more to see, more to be said, more to hear, more to feel, and more to learn than any human being can imagine, and to those who long with me for the Spirit of Truth and Revelation in order to know the Lord Jesus Christ more fully!

Introduction

I chose the title, "Imperceptible Reality" to draw attention to the incredibly broad subject of who God is and what He has created, particularly that which we can't see with our physical eyes. There is undeniably much reality that is imperceptible, and even though a miniscule portion is known by us, I think you'll admit with me that human beings, corporately or individually, don't see *everything*.

If someone actually believed they were so knowledgeable or wise enough to distinguish all that is real, I think they could be compared to a blind man who held one grain of sand in the palm of his hand, thinking he knew exactly what the immense beaches throughout the world were like, even though he never stepped foot on one. Or they could be compared to someone who never tasted a piece of fruit except for a single grape, thinking he knew the flavor of all fruit.

Pause to consider, if God is God, there must be much more than what we can fully grasp. Besides, who would want to worship a god who only knows what we know and has our limitations?

> *Can you fathom the mysteries of God? Can you probe the limits of the Almighty? They are higher than the heavens above—what can you do? They*

*are deeper than the depths below—what can you
know? (Job 11:7-8 NIV).*

Since Adam and Eve, we have been ever learning
and discovering more about our world, and though our
knowledge may seem extensive, it remains slight when
contemplating the universe, the scope of all life, and the
boundless content of eternity. Even Solomon, one of the
wisest men who ever lived, indicated the following:

*He has made everything beautiful in its time.
He has also set eternity in the human heart; yet
no one can fathom what God has done from
beginning to end (Ecclesiastes 3:11 NIV).*

Although we can't see everything, The truth which
we are given in the Bible will help free us from blindness,
deception and ignorance.   In the following chapters, I
attempt to emphasize our great need for faith, growth, and
awareness of the mysterious and magnificent immensity of
God and our relationship to Him.

*Jesus said to the people who believed in him, "You
are truly my disciples if you remain faithful to my
teachings. And you will know the truth, and the
truth will set you free" (John 8:31:32 NLT).*

I pray that as you read the words in this book and study
God's Word, you will experience enlightenment, through
the Holy Spirit, for the Glory of God!

Connie Bertelsen Young

1

IMperceptibLe ReaLity

*Great is the LORD, and highly to be praised,
And His greatness is unsearchable (Psalm 145:3
NASB).*

When I had my eye exam this year, I was a little shocked to find out how much I couldn't easily read on the eye chart, compared to the last time I took a vision test. I definitely needed a new prescription. Having good sight is really important to everyone's life, but I'm sure there is more out there that we *can't* see, than what we *can* see.

Some people have great sight, and they are more perceptive than others. There have been astoundingly brilliant scientists, doctors, leaders, prophets, and teachers in this world since Adam, but none of them have seen or understood *all* there is. This is true even for the geniuses who have scored over the 98th percentile and belong to the Mensa organization. Despite one's intelligence quotient, vast mysteries remain to everyone. Countless things in this universe and beyond are still unidentified and indiscernible.

Throughout the course of time, we've experienced ever-increasing knowledge, found astonishing answers about our world, and observed remarkable things. We've explored our cosmos, accumulated considerable information, developed mind-boggling technology, discovered great things pertaining to our body, soul and spirit, and most importantly, received miraculous revelation through the Word of God. Yet, we see less than the tip of the iceberg.

> *But as it is written: "Eye has not seen, nor ear heard, Nor have entered into the heart of man The things which God has prepared for those who love Him" (1 Corinthians 2:8 NKJV).*

The "Imperceptible Reality" that I refer to herein particularly pertains to the reality of the spiritual world, although there's plenty within the physical world that we have yet to explore or comprehend. In our impaired vision, we can only barely see the meaningfulness of who God is, or what He has accomplished - unbelievers and Christians included.

On the extreme side, those who claim to be atheists may unbendingly say "There is no god." In making that statement, they are indicating that they know everything, and that there cannot be anything greater than what they think they've seen. But the Bible teaches they should not depend on that.

> *Trust in the LORD with all your heart And do*
> *not lean on your own understanding (Proverbs*
> *3:5-8 NASB).*

Still, it is fair to say that even those of us who dogmatically embrace our beliefs in God and the Cross of Christ, find the spiritual world bewildering, and if we're honest, are often unconscious of its certainty. One instance of this, is that we rarely even consider the authenticity of the angels that are all around us. (See Psalm 91:11.)

A.W. Tozer epitomized the problem. "Our trouble is that we have established bad thought habits. We habitually think of the visible world as real and doubt the reality of any other." [1] We miss what is eternal and invisible because we've become over-stimulated, distracted and desensitized by what we can see, hear, taste, touch and smell. That which is eternal and invisible is often disregarded. Unbelievers are particularly insensitive to those things. The Apostle, Paul, gave us a clue with the following words:

> *The person without the Spirit does not accept*
> *the things that come from the Spirit of God*
> *but considers them foolishness, and cannot*
> *understand them because they are discerned*
> *only through the Spirit (1 Corinthians*
> *2:14 NIV).*

Paul was speaking about those who don't have the Spirit within them. He made it clear that we need the Holy Spirit to understand spiritual things, and to be made aware of the spiritual kingdom all around us. Receiving Christ as Savior and being born again begins the Christian journey of spiritual acuity. However, even Christians can become carelessly unconscious of what is here.

I've told this story many times: One spring morning when I was a small child, I remember noticing sunshine pouring through my bedroom window as I made my bed. As I tugged the bedspread in place, I was enchanted to see floating dust particles shining in the air. It amazed me, and I imagined that the dust particles were miniature angels. I was so stunned by my discovery that I called out to my mother. I settled down after Mother gently explained to me that what I was looking at was always everywhere, and but it wasn't visible unless it was reflected by light.

That memory is a good reminder to me. Like perpetual dust particles in the air that surround us all the time, the spirit world is active and real. Unless we have the Light of God, we are oblivious to this reality.

People "feel" spiritual and illuminated in different ways, but glittering feelings are fickle and precarious. Only the enlightenment that comes from the Spirit of God is always trustworthy. Yet, He doesn't show us everything. Jesus told his disciples that He still had things to tell them, but He couldn't tell them everything because they wouldn't be able to bear it. (See John 16:12.) Notwithstanding, He gives enough sight to everyone.

> *For since the creation of the world God's invisible qualities—his eternal power and divine nature—have been clearly seen, being understood from what has been made, so that people are without excuse (Romans 1:20 NIV).*

We have trouble processing and understanding even the visible world, so imagine if we could totally see everything that is hidden from us. Surely, we would be appalled to see how blind, fragile and deceived we are if we saw everything that is true, everything that is real, and everything that is invisible to the human eye.

> *There's far more here than meets the eye. The things we see now are here today, gone tomorrow. But the things we can't see now will last forever (2 Corinthians 4:18 MSG).*

We become short-sighted when our *"mind is set on earthly things."* (See Philippians 3:19 NKJV.) Because of our preoccupation with earthly things, I think most of us have been too narrow with our faith, and we haven't searched the Scriptures as intensively as we ought. (See Hosea 4:6.) There are more than the nominal truths such as God is real and Jesus saved us. Although the fundamentals are highly important, we can develop a broader awareness of eternal things that go beyond a minimal religion. The Holy Spirit and the Word of God can open our spiritual eyes and ears so we don't miss other precious truths.

> *He reveals deep and hidden things; he knows what lies in darkness, and light dwells with him (Daniel 2:22 NIV).*

I've noticed that the pursuit of Holy Ghost experiences may be resisted by some Christians because they fear sensationalism. I dislike the fact that Pentecostals and Charismatics have a bad name in some circles because of some immature and conspicuous behavior observed in a few, causing the more conscientious to shy away from involvement. Others are turned off and resist the move of the Spirit because they find it eerie or weird. Still others struggle because of what God might ask them to do. They fear that God might expect then to give up their seemingly preferable, comfortable life. And He might.

Irrespective of the sincerity and good intentions of those actually led by the Spirit of God and His guidance, some watchers develop adverse biases. This also happened on the day of Pentecost. The people who were filled with the Holy Spirit were observed and mocked by baffled onlookers. (See Acts 2:13.)

Not only do we need to guard ourselves against foolish preconceptions, it is also wise to steer clear of sensationalism, exhibitionism and to be cautious about seeking spiritual manifestations, merely sought for thrill. Nevertheless, unless one is open to God's creativity and revelation, which are new every morning, spiritual receptivity may be blocked by a closed mind. Although I think narrow-mindedness happens to everyone at one time or another, our predispositions can congest and limit us so that we miss the inspiration and spontaneity in a refreshing move of God.

> *We grope like the blind along a wall, feeling our way like people without eyes. Even at brightest noontime, we stumble as though it were dark. Among the living, we are like the dead (Isaiah 59:10 NLT).*

With determination and commitment, we can strengthen our "eyesight" as we abide in Jesus. But again, it's important to guard our appetite and fascination for the supernatural which doesn't pertain to a genuine thirst to know and worship God.

Remember, Simon, the sorcerer, who tried to buy divine ability after watching the apostles ministering in the power of God. (See Acts 8:18-23.) Simon's motivation was not acceptable. There continues to be those illusionists like Simon who bewitch weak-minded individuals by doing the incredible. Speciously, some of those performers think they're doing what is good.

> Many will say to Me in that day, 'Lord, Lord, have we not prophesied in Your name, cast out demons in Your name, and done many wonders in Your name?' And then I will declare to them, 'I never knew you; depart from Me, you who practice lawlessness!' (Matthew 7:22-23 NKJV).

Paul exemplified the only acceptable reason for pursuing spirituality. It is *"so that you may know him better."* (See Ephesians 1:17 NIV.) Like Paul, ambition to be spiritual must come from the desire to fully *know* Christ.

> And we know that the Son of God has come and has given us an understanding, that we may know Him who is true; and we are in Him who is true, in His Son Jesus Christ. This is the true God and eternal life (1 John 5:20 NKJV).

I maintain that the importance of the invisible spiritual world is unrealized by many, even though we have been warned to *"fix our eyes"* on those unseen things that are eternal. (See 2 Corinthians 4:18 NIV.) There is an exciting spiritual "frontier" to be discovered with the help of the Holy Spirit. And there will always be something to learn and see. Our Father continually has something to reveal - if we are willing to look and listen, He will show us.

> For precept must be upon precept, precept upon precept, Line upon line, line upon line, Here a little, there a little (Isaiah 28:10 NKJV).

VISION CHECK FOR CHAPTER 1

1. Read Psalm 147:5. What is the basic difference between human knowledge and God's?

2. Name three things that you believe exist which you have never touched and/or seen with your physical eyes.

3. Read Isaiah 29:14. Explain what you think this passage means.

4. According to 1 Corinthians 1:18, what is the power of God for those who are saved?

5. For what reason do you think that someone would insist that there is no God?

6. Do you personally have evidence that persuades you to believe in some things that cannot be seen with your physical eyes? (See Hebrews 11:1.)

7. According to 2 Corinthians 4:18, should the things we *can't* see or things we *can* see be more important?

2

God Is Here

Where can I go from Your Spirit? Or where can I flee from Your presence? If I ascend to heaven, You are there; If I make my bed in Sheol, behold, You are there. If I take the wings of the dawn, If I dwell in the remotest part of the sea, Even there Your hand will lead me, And Your right hand will lay hold of me. If I say, "Surely the darkness will overwhelm me, And the light around me will be night," Even the darkness is not dark to You, And the night is as bright as the day. Darkness and light are alike to You (Psalm 139:7-12 NASB).

God is omnipresent. That means He is present in all places at the same time. He is existing everywhere, and He is never absent. Still, at times, we might feel like He is more present in certain places than others. Like, we've probably felt His presence more in our churches or in our sanctuaries, than in our shopping centers or in busy traffic. And have you ever felt like God is a million miles away and isn't paying attention? But it doesn't depend on what we feel like. God *is* Here!

After finishing the building of the undoubtedly awe-inspiring temple in Jerusalem, Solomon expressed the following words.

> *But will God indeed dwell on the earth? Behold, heaven and the highest heaven cannot contain You, how much less this house which I have built! (1 Kings 8:27 NASB).*

Solomon knew that God was boundless, and He meditated on that truth.

Acknowledging the Lord's continual presence can certainly change the way we live. Have you have ever wondered if your phone was bugged, or that someone was listening to your conversation and you had to be careful in what you said? Considering the fact that God hears it all, should be a huge influence in all we say and do. Remember, God is always here. Think of the meaning of His name.

> *"Behold, the virgin shall be with child, and bear a Son, and they shall call His name Immanuel," which is translated, "God with us" (Matthew 1:23 NKJV).*

In Hebrews 13:5, Paul reminds us once again that God promised us that He would *never leave us*. With that in mind, we know that God continually accesses our minds, our hearts, and our lives without limits (not just when we feel His presence).

David, very bravely I might add, asked God to check out his heart to see if there was any wickedness there. (See Psalm 139:23-24.) We may attempt to disregard those fleeting wicked thoughts we have, or ignore those relatively small incidences of bad behavior in ourselves, but God doesn't overlook anything that's going on in us.

> *Nothing in all creation is hidden from God's sight. Everything is uncovered and laid bare before the eyes of him to whom we must give account (Hebrews 4:13 NIV).*

Meditate on that verse for a minute. It's kind of scary to recognize that God's sees our every movement, every thought, every word, every pain, every pleasure, and every experience we've ever had or will ever have. He is observing you and me right now.

> *The eyes of the LORD are in every place, Watching the evil and the good (Proverbs 15:3 NASB).*

I think if we could keep that thought in our minds, it would surely make us more conscientious about our responses. Perhaps the reason we forget to consider God's omnipresence is because it is quite astounding to us that Almighty God, Maker of Heaven and earth, bothers to pay such close attention to us individually. Maybe we don't quite believe it.

> *When I consider your heavens, the work of your fingers, the moon and the stars, which you have set in place, what is mankind that you are mindful of them, human beings that you care for them? (Psalm 8:3-4 NIV).*

Or maybe our apparent ignoring of His attentiveness stems from denial. As I indicated, it's unnerving to recognize our bad, and we shudder to think that God sees it all. Nobody likes to admit they keep blowing it - but that isn't a revelation to the Lord.

> *God would surely have known it, for he knows*
> *the secrets of every heart (Psalm 44:21 NLT).*

God made it clear that His presence isn't meant to make us feel condemned in all our obvious misbehavior and guilt (See John 3:17), but rather, He sent His Son to rescue us from our sins and give us life. We find that amazing truth of God's forgiveness unimaginable from a worldly point of view, which insists on paybacks. Our involvement with some of those people who have the "upper hand" in our lives, often because of whatever debt we have to them, rarely results in mercy. But if that experience is all we have to go on, we'll remain impervious to God's Grace. Our eyes must be opened by the Holy Spirit and exposure to the Word, or our hearts won't understand His exceptional generosity.

> *The LORD opens the eyes of the blind; The LORD*
> *raises up those who are bowed down; The LORD*
> *loves the righteous (Psalm 146:8 NASB).*

Enlightenment, for what we desperately need to know, and for that which is true and real (although it may even be invisible), can be experienced through reading and studying the Bible. When we hear the Word of God, it amplifies our awareness of Him in a miraculous way.

> *So then faith comes by hearing, and hearing by*
> *the word of God (Romans 10:17 NKJV).*

The Light of the Word illuminates God's presence. But if we fail to seek Him, we may begin feeling like He is distant.

As children in Sunday School, some of us learned to love the story of Jacob's Ladder. We were told about the patriarch, Jacob, who was very surprised to see God's proximity on one occasion. Before Jacob had that certain eye-opening experience, he may have been unconscious of God's omnipresence. He was totally awestruck when he saw God's holiness divinely revealed to him in an unlikely place. Jacob wasn't in a house of worship, or a religious environment where people expect God to be manifested. Rather, he had been sleeping on the ground, out in the middle of nowhere, with his head on a stone.

> Then Jacob awoke from his sleep and said, "Surely the LORD is in this place, and I wasn't even aware of it!" (Genesis 28:16 NLT).

In Exodus 3:1-6, Moses also had a shocking consciousness of God's presence as he observed an oddly burning bush. This story is another reminder that God has no limitations in where He is. Although related, the manifestation of God is different than His omnipresence, however, He is here, whether or not it is obvious to us, or if we have an extraordinary encounter such as Jacob or Moses had.

I should mention, besides being omnipresent, God is omniscient, which means He has infinite understanding, awareness and insight; furthermore, He is omnipotent, which means He has unlimited power and is able to do anything. He is truly almighty.

> Yours, LORD, is the greatness and the power and the glory and the majesty and the splendor, for

everything in heaven and earth is yours. Yours, LORD, is the kingdom; you are exalted as head over all. Wealth and honor come from you; you are the ruler of all things. In your hands are strength and power to exalt and give strength to all (1 Chronicles 29:11-12 NIV).

The above verse should inspire everyone to want to make the Lord their best friend. Also, because God isn't the only one here that we can't see with our eyes, it would be a good idea to get as close to Him as we possibly can. Our good Shepherd will defend us from our loathsome enemy who roams this planet and works to bring us to ruin.

The thief's purpose is to steal and kill and destroy. My purpose is to give them a rich and satisfying life. "I am the good shepherd. The good shepherd sacrifices his life for the sheep (John 10:10 NLT).

Satan definitely isn't omnipresent, omniscient or omnipotent, but he has power. He particularly tries to manipulate us by poisoning our minds. Then, with our words and actions, we will do one of two things in response. Either we can empower his ability to destroy us and to bring pain and death, or we will cause him to become incapacitated.

Therefore submit to God. Resist the devil and he will flee from you (James 4:7 NKJV).

Because the devil isn't all knowing and all powerful, He can only learn our weaknesses by observing our behavior, and what comes out of our mouth. He is watching for a susceptible target. (See Ephesians 6:16.) Too many people are dangerously ignorant of the reality of demonic influence, and learning to discern the spirits is a much-needed part of the growth process for every born-again believer. (See 1 John 4:1-3).

All across the map, there is appalling wickedness and evil. I often think of the words in the twenty-third Psalm. I'm reminded that even though we walk through the darkness in this world, we don't need to be afraid of evil, because God promises to never leave us.

> O LORD, You have searched me and known me. You know when I sit down and when I rise up; You understand my thought from afar. You scrutinize my path and my lying down, And are intimately acquainted with all my ways. Even before there is a word on my tongue, Behold, O LORD, You know it all. You have enclosed me behind and before, And laid Your hand upon me. Such knowledge is too wonderful for me; It is too high, I cannot attain to it (Psalm 139:1-6 NASB).

VISION CHECK FOR CHAPTER 2

1. Read Job 28:24. Name a place or situation where people might think that God isn't there, or that He doesn't see what's happening.

2. Can you recount a time in your life when you thought God was distant, or that He didn't seem available?

3. Read Deuteronomy 31:8. What does this verse show about God's presence in your personal life?

4. How can reading the Bible bring reassurance that God is here? (See Romans 10:17.)

5. Has there been a special time in your life when you felt God's presence to be especially profound?

6. According to 1 John 4:1-3, how can we recognize the Spirit of God?

7. List one thing that we do not wrestle against, and four things that we should. (See Ephesians 6:12.)

8. Read Psalm 33:13-15. Who is God watching?

3

God Manifested

Seraphim stood above Him, each having six wings: with two he covered his face, and with two he covered his feet, and with two he flew. And one called out to another and said, "Holy, Holy, Holy, is the LORD of hosts, The whole earth is full of His glory" (Isaiah 6:2-3 NASB).

I've met missionaries who have seen some spectacular miracles. To mention a few things, they tell of seeing things like broken bones set back in place, empty gas tanks filled, cancerous growths disappearing, sight given to the blind, provision, healing and other tremendous answers to prayers of faith.

Admittedly, I've not had much experience in observing such spine-tingling miracles as that, but I've often thought,

I'd like to see God do something really sensational so people could see His mighty power. Maybe then unbelievers would come to worship Him.

> *Summon your might, O God. Display your power, O God, as you have in the past (Psalm 68:28 NLT).*

I was reminded of the Pharisees that tested Jesus and demanded a sign from Him because they wanted Him to prove His authority (see Mark 8:11 and John 2:18). Although He could have given them what they wanted, we learn that this wasn't the way Jesus operated. He loved people so intensely that He died to save them - but He wasn't a people-pleaser.

In Luke 16:19-31, Jesus told the story about a rich man who lived a life of luxury in the presence of Lazarus, who was a poor beggar. Both men died and the beggar was carried to Heaven, but the rich man ended up in Hades. Then the rich man begged for Lazarus to go to his living brothers and warn them to change their ways so they wouldn't also end up in torment. The story concluded with the fact that, those who don't listen to Moses and the Prophets, won't even be convinced if someone is risen from the dead.

I have realized that a dramatic show of power actually isn't what it takes to convert people. Besides, the whole world is full of miracles that go unnoticed, and which we take for granted most of the time. Ronald Reagan was quoted as saying, "God's miracles are to be found in nature itself; the wind and waves, the wood that becomes a tree – all of these are explained biologically, but behind them is the hand of God." [2]

God is manifested in sundry ways. One way He does this is through what He created (see Romans 1:19-20). Also, He always manifests Himself through love (see John 14:21), and through believers (see 2 Corinthians 4:11). Primarily, and ultimately, God is manifested through Christ. In John 14:9, Jesus explained to Philip that anyone who has seen Jesus, has also seen God.

Maybe you've noticed that some people are inclined to have inflexible ideas about how God, could, or could not, be manifested today. But if they are unbending about this, they must not realize that God can do whatever He wants.

I like the following simple definition. "When something is manifest, it is evident, obvious, apparent, and plain for everyone to see." [3]

It's apparent that God chooses to manifest His power differently than the way the world typically presents anything of interest. Instead of noisy, flashy exhibitions that dazzle and demand our attention in order to get a point across, He has spoken clearly, in a still, small voice.

God has chosen unadorned purity and uncomplicated truth. It's unfortunate that most of us have become disproportionately beguiled by earthly charm, instead of looking and listening more carefully for Him.

> But I am afraid that, as the serpent deceived Eve by his craftiness, your minds will be led astray from the simplicity and purity of devotion to Christ (2 Corinthians 11:3 NASB).

Rather than allowing ourselves to be spellbound by the illustrious, external prettiness or grandiose displays, we can learn to watch for that which is lowly, peaceful, and perhaps even seemingly plain, since those are often godly features.

Remember the idiom: "Don't judge a book by its cover." This means "you shouldn't make a judgement about someone or something – be it a book or otherwise-based solely on its outward appearance."[4] The world customarily gives adoration to the "cover," but exteriors give an incomplete perspective. It's foolish to evaluate anything by a mere facade, however beautiful. Human appraisals are unlike God's assessments.

> *But God chose the foolish things of the world to shame the wise; God chose the weak things of the world to shame the strong. God chose the lowly things of this world and the despised things—and the things that are not—to nullify the things that are (1 Corinthians 1:27-28 NIV).*

The prophet, Samuel, thought that God would likely choose to anoint and manifest Himself through someone who looked good to be the King of Israel. Instead, the less impressive, shepherd boy, David, was God's choice.

> *When they arrived, Samuel saw Eliab and thought, "Surely the LORD's anointed stands here before the LORD." But the LORD said to Samuel, "Do not consider his appearance or his height, for I have rejected him. The LORD does not look at the things people look at. People look at the outward appearance, but the LORD looks at the heart" (1 Samuel 16:6-7 NIV).*

Humans are generally more likely to pay attention to the best-looking individuals. It's interesting that Jesus wasn't especially striking in His physical appearance. I guess the consideration for His physical appeal didn't have any bearing on the One who fashioned His body.

He grew up before him like a tender shoot, and like a root out of dry ground. He had no beauty or majesty to attract us to him, nothing in his appearance that we should desire him. He was despised and rejected by mankind, a man of suffering, and familiar with pain. Like one from whom people hide their faces he was despised, and we held him in low esteem (Isaiah 53:2-3 NIV).

Although we haven't seen much glamour or pizzazz in how God operates, there will be an unmistakably, mind-blowing, electrifying day when Jesus returns. The most spectacular, blazing firework show we've ever seen, or the most dazzling, astonishing electric light event that people have ever bought tickets to see, will look like nothing in comparison to what we all will be seeing (for free) on the day when Jesus appears.

For as the lightning comes from the east and flashes to the west, so also will the coming of the Son of Man be (Matthew 24:27 NKJV).

Meanwhile, until that day, it is through faith that we are assured of things not seen, even if we haven't yet attended a divine presentation of miraculous manifestation. Anyway, we should probably be more interested in the better blessings that Jesus spoke about in the following verse.

Jesus said, "So, you believe because you've seen with your own eyes. Even better blessings are in store for those who believe without seeing" (John 20:29 MSG).

I don't know about you, but most of the time I find it easiest for my faith to rise higher on Sunday morning, when I'm sitting in church, worshipping with other believers. It probably shouldn't be that way, but frankly, inspiration usually diminishes somewhat during the week as I do mundane things. Driving in heavy traffic, paying my bills or cleaning toilets are definitely not very divine experiences.

Although we inhabit the spiritual world along with the natural world, we have a tendency to divide them, and make them separate in our mentality. Grace Livingston Hill told of her uninterrupted relationship with the Lord when she wrote, "It is my joy that He has not separated any moment of my life from Him saying, 'Here is so much drudgery each day, from which I must be entirely separated; then, when that is done, you may serve me.'"[5]

> *Whether, then, you eat or drink or whatever you do, do all to the glory of God (1 Corinthians 10:31 NASB).*

"Whatever" includes those objectionable mundane tasks I mentioned. No matter how diverse our lifestyles may be, with pleasures, hardships, habits, working, sleeping, eating, etc., we can *do all to the glory of God*. Then He will be noticeable, through us, for everyone to see.

It's no coincidence that missionaries are often the ones who tell of astonishing miracles. With outstanding faith, many have trusted God by leaving their comfortable homes to minister in impoverished countries. Nevertheless, miracles should be anticipated by all believers. It is through the faith of believers that God will manifest Himself.

> *These miraculous signs will accompany those who believe: They will cast out demons in my name, and they will speak in new languages (Mark 16:17 NLT).*

Faithful, Holy Spirit filled Christians are a means for which God shows Himself. This is a huge responsibility for Christians to represent Him. (See Romans 10:14.) When we celebrate The Lord's Supper, we're reminded of the necessity of receiving The Bread of Life, because it is only through His life that we can manifest life.

> *And he took bread, gave thanks and broke it, and gave it to them, saying, "This is my body given for you; do this in remembrance of me" (Luke 22:19 NIV).*

God is manifested first through Christ, who is the Head of the Church, but also through the Church, which is His Body. (See 1 Corinthians 12:27.) As God manifested Himself through the flesh of Jesus, He will manifest Himself through those who partake of Christ.

> *But anyone who eats my flesh and drinks my blood has eternal life, and I will raise that person at the last day. For my flesh is true food, and my blood is true drink. Anyone who eats my flesh and drinks my blood remains in me, and I in him. I live because of the living Father who sent me; in the same way, anyone who feeds on me will live because of me (John 6:54-57 NLT).*

VISION CHECK FOR CHAPTER 3

1. Many believed in Jesus when they saw the signs He did
    (see John 2:23), but do you think people usually come to
    belief in God by simply witnessing a miracle?

2. According to 1 John 5:10, what must everyone do to
    believe?

3. What does Zechariah 4:6 show is not, and also show
    what is, the source of getting great tasks accomplished?

4. Have your first impressions of someone or something turned out to be incorrect once you had more information, and why is measuring worth by human reasoning and outside appearance often unreliable? (See Isaiah 55:8-9.)

5. How is God manifested through those who have received Christ as Savior? (See 2 Corinthians 4:10.)

6. (Read James 5:16.) What can you do to help bring about the divine healing of a body or soul?

7. According to John 14:21, to whom does God choose to reveal Himself?

BLINDNESS

Satan, who is the god of this world, has blinded the minds of those who don't believe. They are unable to see the glorious light of the Good News. They don't understand this message about the glory of Christ, who is the exact likeness of God (2 Corinthians 4:4 NLT).

The seductive god of this world continually attempts to blind and captivate humanity with his charms, and it's not merely the unsaved who are vulnerable to blindness. He entices everybody with countless alluring things that tempt and distract, so we won't see clearly. The enemy knows what things can change our focus and sway us. And when he succeeds in blindsiding us, we are as vulnerable as sheep who move away from the protection of the Shepherd, into the savage wolf's territory.

You are my rock and my fortress. For the honor of your name, lead me out of this danger. Pull me from the trap my enemies set for me, for I find protection in you alone (Psalm 31:3-4 NLT).

Even when we think we're not susceptible to the wolf, He is always trying to slyly lure us to his trap by appealing to our human appetite. Even though those enticements, whatever they may be, might seem harmless enough, we will suffer the consequences whenever we are moving away from obedience to the Lord. Then, our sight is blurred in a haze of the temporary gratification the wolf offers, and we aren't as cognizant of the danger that we're in. True blindness is when we are not able to see our neediness for the Lord's rescue.

You say, 'I am rich. I have everything I want. I don't need a thing!' And you don't realize that you are wretched and miserable and poor and blind and naked (Revelation 3:17 NLT).

It's human nature to want to feel secure, and there isn't anything wrong with that in itself, but putting our trust in the world, or anything and anybody other than God, will eventually bring disappointment. (See Isaiah 31:1.) Of course, it is wise to try to be well prepared, but materialistic preparations are the least important for security, because despite all our fleshly provisions and arrangements, we are still blind to the future.

Why, you do not even know what will happen tomorrow. What is your life? You are a mist that appears for a little while and then vanishes (James 4:14 NIV).

The best preparation has little to do with things like our household necessities, our bank accounts, investments, insurance policies and job security. Although they may be an important part of good stewardship, these things can be quickly changed or removed from us. Nor can our government and leaders, our family, or other people in our lives, make us secure. Because of our impaired vision, our safekeeping ultimately depends on the only One who sees the whole procession of our lives, from birth to death.

> How great is the goodness you have stored up for those who fear you. You lavish it on those who come to you for protection, blessing them before the watching world. You hide them in the shelter of your presence, safe from those who conspire against them. You shelter them in your presence, far from accusing tongues (Psalm 31:19-20 NLT).

I have a large map of the world on the wall of my home office. The illustrations representing continents, islands and bodies of water on this map are shown in relatively small proportion. Although the map provides me with some perception of the world, that map is smaller than the area of ground where I have tomato plants growing in my back yard. If that puny map was all I have to visualize the world, my concept would be extremely limited. The map doesn't show me ocean waves mounting, the sun rising, wind blowing in the trees, snowflakes falling, stars twinkling, or millions of other features of the real world.

Likening the inadequacy of that map for giving a complete understanding of the natural world, to the insufficiency of our sight of the spiritual world, is just a reminder of our inability to see perfectly, and to consider all that's unseen. Yet I must admit, this analogy is actually a poor comparison when it comes to our attempts at grasping all that Almighty God has created.

> *We know only a portion of the truth, and what we say about God is always incomplete (1 Corinthians 13:9 MSG).*

The Bible provides something so much better than a mere map of the world. The Word of God is divine information that will deliver us from ignorance and give us hope, so that we can learn how to live. Then we can better see what we are and understand what is coming. (See 2 Timothy 3:16.) But like the map on my wall which gives us only a little indication of the real world, we still can't see everything.

> *Now we see things imperfectly as in a cloudy mirror, but then we will see everything with perfect clarity. All that I know now is partial and incomplete, but then I will know everything completely, just as God now knows me completely (1 Corinthians 13:12 NLT).*

Someday, perfect sight will be ours. We won't need a library card to access the information that we once searched for in books, we won't be turning to Google every time we need an answer to our many questions, and we won't be stumped in making the right decisions. But meanwhile, we can't see much. We're in good company with Job in Old Testament times who finally acknowledged his poor eyesight. We can identify with Him and smile at the following translation of his words in the Message Bible.

> *You asked, 'Who is this muddying the water,*
> *ignorantly confusing the issue, second-guessing*
> *my purposes?' I admit it. I was the one. I babbled*
> *on about things far beyond me, made small talk*
> *about wonders way over my head. You told*
> *me, 'Listen, and let me do the talking. Let me*
> *ask the questions. You give the answers' (Job*
> *42:3-4 MSG).*

At one time or another when we see suffering, most of us have probably said or thought, "Why would God let this happen?" We may feel like we're entitled to an answer. We may even think we know what is deserved or not deserved; however, again, we need to remember we are regularly blind to God's flawless purposes and judgments.

Perhaps you know someone who formerly attended church who became disgruntled, and then turned away, refusing to go back because of something that they thought was unfair. I suppose we've all had times when we felt like running away, for whatever reason. That's exactly what the devil wants us to do.

As I've said before, I personally believe that when we see and experience hardships and suffering, "We really shouldn't insinuate that 'life is not fair,' because that implies that God is not fair." [6] Rather, we can trust that everything is in His Hand.

> *And we know that all things work together for*
> *good to those who love God, to those who are*
> *called according to His purpose (Romans 8:28*
> *NKJV).*

Remembering that God can use everything happening to us for our benefit, can help keep us from falling into despair, even in the darkest of times. However, our imperfect sight still makes us vulnerable to our enemies and those things which can destroy us – and those things aren't always obvious. For the most part, our worst adversaries are rarely visible. (See 2 Corinthians 11:14.) Knowing the Word, and relying on God to protect and lead us, is critical to our safety. Turning with all our hearts to God and making Jesus Lord of our lives is the first step in achieving clarity.

> *Trust in the LORD with all your heart, And lean not on your own understanding; In all your ways acknowledge Him, And He shall direct your paths. Do not be wise in your own eyes; Fear the LORD and depart from evil (Proverbs 3:5-7 NKJV).*

We are most blind when we think we're wise enough to handle everything. (See Romans 12:3.) An attitude of self-sufficiency and pride can make truth very indistinctive.

> *The way of the wicked is like darkness; They do not know over what they stumble (Proverbs 4:19 NASB).*

There are culprits which will obscure our vision, but we can't continue repeating the excuse saying "The devil made me do it"[7] like Flip Wilson's character, Geraldine, used to say. Among other things, entertaining things like hatred, unforgiveness, self-pity, laziness, gluttony and selfishness can cause terrible blindness. In general, sin is the epitome of why we lose direction and can't see the right way to go. (See Isaiah 59:2.) Poor eyesight is perpetuated by bad choices, and wrong turns lead to dead ends.

See to it that no one takes you captive through philosophy and empty deception, according to the tradition of men, according to the elementary principles of the world, rather than according to Christ (Colossians 2:8 NASB).

Beginning with our essential relationship to Jesus Christ, I think relationships are the most important thing in our lives. Our relationships have a profound influence on us, and it's normal to pick up our friends' opinions, habits, language and ideas – making it necessary to be cautious in our associations. Swiss psychiatrist and psychoanalyst, Carl Gustav Jung, said "The meeting of two personalities is like the contact of two chemical substances: if there is any reaction, both are transformed."[8]

There are many Bible verses advising us about our relationships. Among them, we are warned not to keep company with evil people because our behavior can be corrupted; we are never supposed to be teamed up with people who aren't Christians, and we are to avoid those who cause division. The Apostle Paul tearfully warned us to be vigilant. (See Acts 20:29-31.)

Through the mercy of God, we no longer have to walk in darkness because Jesus opens the eyes of the blind. 1 Peter 2:9 tells us he has called us to come into His marvelous light.

If we say that we have fellowship with Him and yet walk in the darkness, we lie and do not practice the truth; but if we walk in the Light as He Himself is in the Light, we have fellowship with one another, and the blood of Jesus His Son cleanses us from all sin (1 John 1:6-7 NASB).

﷽

VISION CHECK FOR CHAPTER 4

1. When will everyone's eyes be opened? (See Isaiah 35:4-5.)

2. According to Matthew 13:15, why can't people see?

3. Read 1 John 2:11 and tell what can make a person blind?

4. What will every human see at last when Christ comes? (See Luke 3:6.)

5. How are spiritual realities understood? (See 1 Corinthians 2:10-13.)

6. Read Psalm 1:1. Name something which could lead you to have wrong thinking?

7. According to Isaiah 59:2, how can sin affect receiving answers to our prayers?

5

AWaKeNiNg

But you, brothers and sisters, are not in darkness so that this day should surprise you like a thief. You are all children of the light and children of the day. We do not belong to the night or to the darkness. So then, let us not be like others, who are asleep, but let us be awake and sober (1 Thessalonians 5:4-6 NIV).

Although I get up very early in the morning, my husband can tell you, I'm not really a morning person. My body sort of moves automatically out of necessity when I get out of bed, but it takes a while before the lights in my brain become bright. Waking up is a slow process for me. I can compare this fact to my spiritual awakening. It took a long time before I could see the Grace of God and commit my life fully to Christ, even though I was exposed to Christianity at an early age. But I'm awake and growing now.

Like waking up from sleep, waking up to the truth is a different process for all of us, and not everyone has the same experience. In Matthew 13:18-23, we read the Parable of the Sower and learn about a variety of human responses to the Good News of Salvation. I think we may identify with most of them, at least a little bit at one time or another.

First, there are those who don't understand God's message to them, so they don't develop faith. Other personalities hear the Word and are enthusiastic about it, but they soon fall away. Then there are the ones who have too much wealth, which sidetracks them. The best response in the parable was the one who listened and understood and lived a productive life.

Today, you have a choice to how you will respond to the Word which is sowed. I hope you will make the best choice (see James 1:21), and determine to grow and develop a strong faith, so that your life will flourish.

> *Incline your ear and hear the words of the wise, And apply your heart to my knowledge; For it is a pleasant thing if you keep them within you; Let them all be fixed upon your lips, So that your trust may be in the LORD; I have instructed you today, even you (Proverbs 22:17-19 NKJV).*

As we study God's Word and listen to the Holy Spirit, we find there is always more wisdom and knowledge to grasp and apply every day. Yet maybe you've noticed, although sometimes God's revelation seems to come easily to you, or at just the perfect time, while at other times, you may feel like you're living in fog without direction or inspiration. But remember, Jesus promised that those who *hunger and thirst for righteousness* will be filled.

I've learned that enlightenment usually comes to me at the speed I sincerely seek Him. Admittedly, I'm afraid I've had too many "slow" days. (See Hebrews 12:1.)

> *When you come looking for me, you'll find me. Yes, when you get serious about finding me and want it more than anything else (Jeremiah 29:13 MSG).*

If we neglect looking for the Lord, we can miss out on the wonderful things He is waiting to show us. Christian author and speaker, Lisa Terkeurst, wrote, "We have become so familiar with God yet so unaware of Him."[9] Yes, we may know in our heads that He is indeed always with us, but if we become sedated in our response to the reality of His presence, something is wrong and we need to wake up. Although our relationship to the Lord isn't based on emotions, surely, we would feel a little excitement acknowledging that God is nearby.

> *Tremble, Earth! You're in the Lord's presence! in the presence of Jacob's God (Psalm 114:7 MSG).*

As I've repeatedly indicated, the world can lull us to sleep with distractions that can desensitize us to what's important. It can blur our focus, and cause us to sleepily shut our eyes to God if we aren't careful. It's hazardous to settle into worldly indifference. When we allow this to happen, we are vulnerable to backsliding into sin.

> *So let's not sleepwalk through life like those others. Let's keep our eyes open and be smart (1 Thessalonians 5:6 MSG).*

As Christians, we need to be rooted and grounded in right priorities. Being able to control our thinking and keeping ourselves alert is a basic indication of maturity. When temptation comes, and it will come, we have the power to change our minds. The Bible shows us how to do this.

> Finally, brothers and sisters, whatever is true, whatever is noble, whatever is right, whatever is pure, whatever is lovely, whatever is admirable— if anything is excellent or praiseworthy—think about such things (Philippians 4:8 NIV).

We can stay awake and be in perfect peace by keeping our mind on Jesus. (See Isaiah 26:3.) Putting our relationship with Jesus first in everything, is the most important consideration of our lives. Until He is Lord, we will be somnambulating through life.

> "Teacher, which is the great commandment in the law?" Jesus said to him, "'You shall love the LORD your God with all your heart, with all your soul, and with all your mind' (Matthew 22:36-37 NKJV).

There are other words which I could have used in place of "Awakening," for the title and emphasis of this chapter. For instance, verbs such as "developing," "growing" and "arising" would also be appropriate for the subject. Those words imply movement - and loving God requires wakeful action.

An apathetic attitude, has no place in the very real battle going on all around us. A soldier can't sleep in a war zone. Imagine missiles, bombs and other destructive elements bursting all around him. I don't believe he would be behaving nonchalantly. In comparison, it seems many people are oblivious to the spiritual war that is going on, while lives are ruined by an invisible enemy.

> *For we do not wrestle against flesh and blood, but against principalities, against powers, against the rulers of the darkness of this age, against spiritual hosts of wickedness in the heavenly places (Ephesians 6:12 NKJV.)*

The battle is ongoing, and the awakening that God has for us isn't dependent upon anyone but ourselves. I'm afraid that living in this world, which is so full of sensational stimulants, has caused us to become accustomed to looking outward for something to motivate us. For instance, sometimes we look to the Church to arouse us. Of course, we want the message and the music to convince and inspire us - but the problem is when we forget to take responsibility for our own development.

> *Consider and hear me, O LORD my God; Enlighten my eyes, Lest I sleep the sleep of death (Psalm 13:3 NKJV).*

I once had the idealistic attitude of thinking that the right church, the wise counselor, or the special relationship could somehow solve my problems, and give me the guidance and encouragement that I felt I sorely needed. But I had to wake up to the truth. The final answers aren't from human beings or the natural world.

> *I took my troubles to the LORD; I cried out to him, and he answered my prayer (Psalm 120:1 NLT).*

Meanwhile, it will be the imperfect situations in our lives that will help to make and mold us. During the times when we aren't experiencing difficulties, we don't reach out to the Lord as much. We usually become more serious about getting His help in the hard times - and that's when we grow the most.

If our lives are truly submitted to the Will of God, He will lead us precisely where we need to be, and He will open and close doors accordingly. Meanwhile, He is our supplier for everything. (See Philippians 4:19.) We don't have to wait impatiently for that often longed for response from a mere human. Besides, people can't really ever completely understand our needs anyway, even if they do offer some comfort.

> *But you have received the Holy Spirit, and he lives within you, so you don't need anyone to teach you what is true. For the Spirit teaches you everything you need to know, and what he teaches is true—it is not a lie. So just as he has taught you, remain in fellowship with Christ (1 John 2:27 NLT).*

It's the one in our mirror who is responsible for our awakening. Each of us, individually, has the task of digging out the truth, resisting the lies of the enemy and pursuing God. (See 2 Timothy 2:15.)

We can prepare our eyes to see Him by surrendering ourselves each morning while we're still in bed, as soon as we wake from sleep. This can be a lifechanging habit. Then as we diligently and prayerfully study the Bible, looking to Him each day, He will teach us what we need to know.

For the light makes everything visible. This is why it is said, "Awake, O sleeper, rise up from the dead, and Christ will give you light" (Ephesians 5:14 NLT).

I remember as a child when I went back to sleep after I turned off my alarm clock, my dad would throw a pillow at me so I would wake up and get ready for school on time. Today, we've heard the spiritual "alarm clock," and I believe our Father God is giving us a nudge to wake us up - so we will be ready on time.

"When the Son of Man returns, it will be like it was in Noah's day. In those days before the flood, the people were enjoying banquets and parties and weddings right up to the time Noah entered his boat. People didn't realize what was going to happen until the flood came and swept them all away. That is the way it will be when the Son of Man comes (Matthew 24:37-39 NLT).

VISION CHECK FOR CHAPTER 5

1. What will happen to those who ignore God? (See Jeremiah 2:19.)

2. Read Acts 17:28. According to this verse, how far is God from us?

3. What are we promised, if we do what it says in Matthew 6:33?

4. Explain if you have ever identified with any of the responses of those described in the Parable of the Sower in Matthew 13:18-23.

5. Read Luke 10:21. To whom does God give revelation?

6. In Numbers 21:8, What did the Israelites have to do in order to live, and how do you think this verse is relative to our awakening?

7. List some of the things that Psalm 19:7-10 promises that the Word of God will do.

6

priorities

And do not lead us into temptation, But deliver us from the evil one. For Yours is the kingdom and the power and the glory forever. Amen (Matthew 6:13 NKJV).

Sometimes life feels like a juggling act. With so many options, we're always trying to figure out the best way to use our time, our money and our resources. Lots of good opportunities may present themselves, but we have to choose how to respond to them. And the fact is, we only have so much time to do what is right.

> *I do want to point out, friends, that time is of the essence. There is no time to waste, so don't complicate your lives unnecessarily. Keep it simple—in marriage, grief, joy, whatever. Even in*

> *ordinary things—your daily routines of shopping,*
> *and so on. Deal as sparingly as possible with the*
> *things the world thrusts on you. This world as you*
> *see it is on its way out (1 Corinthians 7:29-31 MSG).*

You may have heard something like this before: When contrasted with eternity, you could think of this life as a single grain of sand compared to eternal life, with eternity represented metaphorically by the complete collection of all the grains of sand on beaches, ocean floors and coastlines of the whole world, multiplied centillion times centillions. Although that still doesn't help us to fully comprehend eternity, maybe it will help us remember that this life is relatively, very, very short.

> *Our days on earth are like grass; like wildflowers,*
> *we bloom and die. The wind blows, and we are*
> *gone— as though we had never been here (Psalm*
> *103:15-16 NLT).*

For a while, in the here and now, we make choices which will obviously affect the outcome of what happens to us in this life; however, those decisions that we make **now** will have a much lengthier significance in the hereafter. I've probably understated that fact, because if we consider the implications of a mere 70-80 years (more or less) of living now, versus time without end, we can conclude that the words "lengthier significance" is rather inadequate terminology. Unfortunately, I lack the vocabulary to show the supreme importance and urgency for each of us to make the right choices **today.** The Word of God encourages best.

> *For the world offers only a craving for physical*
> *pleasure, a craving for everything we see, and*

> *pride in our achievements and possessions.*
> *These are not from the Father, but are from this*
> *world. And this world is fading away, along with*
> *everything that people crave. But anyone who*
> *does what pleases God will live forever (1 John*
> *2:16-17 NLT).*

Since we are promised that we will be rewarded for our good works, it should give us incentive for choosing well. The problem with that is only when people think their good works are earning their way to Heaven. Jesus already paid the high cost of entry so we could be in right standing with God. But being generous to us, He not only paid the price of our admission to Heaven and forgave us of our wrong doings, He promised to reward us, for whatever good things we do for Him in this life, before we get there. The fabulous generosity and love of God is never ending, yet somehow, the kindness and simplicity of His plan for everyone's blessing is often disregarded and remains unaccepted by many.

> *Look, I am coming soon! My reward is with me,*
> *and I will give to each person according to what*
> *they have done (Revelation 22:12 NIV).*

Have you ever given serious thought to the reward that you might have? Maybe like me, you've taken time to analyze your labor, and realized that on that inevitable day when God will bring your motives to light, (or I could say, lights them up) there might only be ashes left for your fruitless efforts. I hope that's not the case!

> *Now if anyone builds on this foundation with*
> *gold, silver, precious stones, wood, hay, straw,*

*each one's work will become clear; for the Day
will declare it, because it will be revealed by fire;
and the fire will test each one's work, of what
sort it is. If anyone's work which he has built on
it endures, he will receive a reward. If anyone's
work is burned, he will suffer loss; but he himself
will be saved, yet so as through fire (1 Corinthians
3:12-15 NKJV).*

As long as we're alive, we can build a reward, and we need to establish priorities and pursue goals in our attempts to do that. Being specific in managing our time on this earth will make a positive difference, not only in the afterlife, but also in our lives on this very day. Robert H. Schuller said, "Goals are not only absolutely necessary to motivate us. They are crucial to really keep us alive."[10]

Pursuing a dream can inspire and give us purpose to face a new day, but little is accomplished by people who don't have a goal for their dream. Having goals helps to give us reason to get out of bed in the morning. On the other hand, the root of boredom and depression grows in people who haven't figured out what they need to do. They tend to sleepwalk along in life without incentive, hoping that they might bump into inspiration or purpose, not recognizing that it must be developed by themselves.

Frankly, I'm guilty of using the excuse of "I'm too busy" to do certain positive things that I could do. But curiously, and like everyone else, I generally seem to find the time to do what I really want to do. So, that's why I occasionally need to do an inventory of what I'm doing with my time. Then I can also review my goals, because sometimes they need adjustment. Maybe the goal is unrealistically high or set too low.

My lists of goals help me stick with them. Short-term goals could be things like cleaning out a closet, sending a thank you note, visiting a neighbor or washing my windows. Examples of long-term goals might pertain to things like budgeting expenditures, developing certain relationships, building a savings account or changing eating behaviors. Some people have a "bucket list," itemizing those things that want to accomplish before they die. Other people are more interested in health considerations or changing their lifestyles. Experts say it can take anywhere from 18 to 254 days for most people to form a new habit,[11] although there are differing opinions about how long it actually takes. In the meantime, the Holy Spirit is the central one in the ability to achieve any goal, because success depends heavily on self-control, a fruit of the Spirit.

> A person without self-control is like a city with broken-down walls (Proverbs 25:28 NLT).

I believe God has endowed every human with a unique dream that can lead us to His meaningful, purpose and priority. His design may lay dormant in those who don't seek God's Will for their life, but those who endeavor to follow after His plan will be fulfilled.

> For I know the plans that I have for you,' declares the LORD, 'plans for welfare and not for calamity to give you a future and a hope (Jeremiah 29:11 NASB).

It begins with prioritizing. For instance, when the Lord calls a man or woman into a particular work or ministry, there are likely to be activities or things that deplete their strength or focus that need to be laid down, in order to give more attention to the primary purpose. Sacrifice may be necessary in the pursuit of the greater treasure.

> *Again, the kingdom of heaven is like a merchant seeking beautiful pearls, who, when he had found one pearl of great price, went and sold all that he had and bought it (Matthew 13:45-46 NKJV).*

When we clutter our time with many nonessentials, we find ourselves going in circles without accomplishing much. To evaluate our resources and use them well is good stewardship. One dictionary explains, "Someone's stewardship of something is the way in which they control or take care of it."[12] Ideally, the priority of our stewardship should be using what God gives us to minister to others. (See 1 Peter 4:10.)

> *"I have the right to do anything," you say—but not everything is beneficial. "I have the right to do anything"—but not everything is constructive. No one should seek their own good, but the good of others (1 Corinthians 10:23-24 NIV).*

When Jesus spoke of the greatest commandment, He made it clear that loving God and loving others is primary. And everything that we have is distributed to us for the purpose of bringing glory to God. Until that priority is established in our hearts, the fulfillment of our unique calling might be unrealized.

> *Now he who supplies seed to the sower and bread for food will also supply and increase your store of seed and will enlarge the harvest*

> *of your righteousness. You will be enriched in
> every way so that you can be generous on every
> occasion, and through us your generosity will
> result in thanksgiving to God (2 Corinthians
> 9:10-11 NIV).*

There are really no coincidences. Whatever is happening, and our decisions and response to what is happening, might seem insignificant. Nevertheless, although some things are less important, everything works together for good of those who love God. Author, Amy Carmichael, who for twenty years was confined to her room in constant pain, determined to glorify God by making it her priority to maintain a right spirit. She wrote, "Everything is important, even the tiniest thing."[13]

Our attitudes and motives for doing even small things, have significance as to whether we will bring glory to God. It would be wise for us to frequently check our motives. (See James 4:3 and 1 Corinthians 10:31.) Anything we do for the glory of God builds a reward. John Maxwell said, "Doing the right thing daily, compounds over time."[14]

We all have a treasury. It's often worldly stuff like what's in our houses, our garages or our wallet – but those things won't last forever. Thankfully, there is a safe place of storage for the real treasure.

> *Sell your possessions and give to the poor. Provide
> purses for yourselves that will not wear out, a
> treasure in heaven that will never fail, where no
> thief comes near and no moth destroys (Luke
> 12:33 NIV).*

Sticking with right priorities is "where the rubber meets the road" in a Christian's life. When we are faced with (inevitable) temptation, we are vulnerable to failure, unless a righteous mindset has been established. It helps to solidify our choice to obey God in all circumstances beforehand, and He will provide an escape from wickedness. (See 1 Corinthians 10:13.)

> *Command those who are rich in this present world not to be arrogant nor to put their hope in wealth, which is so uncertain, but to put their hope in God, who richly provides us with everything for our enjoyment. Command them to do good, to be rich in good deeds, and to be generous and willing to share. In this way they will lay up treasure for themselves as a firm foundation for the coming age, so that they may take hold of the life that is truly life (1 Timothy 6:17-19 NIV).*

VISION CHECK FOR CHAPTER 6

1. Has God given you a dream of something you could do with your life, and if so, how is Matthew 16:24-25 related to the end result?

2. List two short-term goals that you could reach in two months or less, and one long-term goal you'd like to reach in approximately one to five years.

3. Read Ecclesiastes 3:1-17. What do you think this passage could be saying about what you do or not do with your time?

4. What were two of Solomon's priorities? (See 2 Chronicles 1:7-11.)

5. Author, Stephen Covey wrote, "Most of us spend too much time on what is urgent and not enough time on what is important."[15] Can you think of something for which you may be spending too much of your time?

6. Read Luke 12:19-21. What are we warned about in these verses, and what do you think it means to be rich toward God?

7. The phrase "You can't take it with you" is a reminder that we can't keep any of our money or possessions when we die; however, according to Revelation 14:13, what goes with us?

7

Deception

Be alert and of sober mind. Your enemy the devil prowls around like a roaring lion looking for someone to devour (1 Peter 5:8 NIV).

When things are going well and life is moving smoothly, it's easy to forget that our enemy is always hiding from our sight, and waiting for an opportunity to destroy us. (See John 10:10.) We tend to let down our guard when things feel comfortable and safe.

He who trusts in his own heart is a fool, But he who walks wisely will be delivered (Proverbs 28:26 NASB).

We might get to feeling self-sufficient, but we are especially fragile when we feel that way. The devil is happy for us to think we have everything figured out, and he likes us to think we have a tight hold on things. The truth is, those who don't relinquish the control of their lives to the Lord are most vulnerable. The Psalmist knew the only place of safety.

> *Keep me safe, my God, for in you I take refuge*
> *(Psalm 16:1 NIV).*

Before he met Jesus on the Road to Damascus, the Apostle Paul behaved boldly and confidently, audaciously thinking he knew what was right. He hated all the followers of Christ and was zealous in his religious thinking. He was convinced that what the believers in Jesus were saying was completely false.

> *Meanwhile, Saul was still breathing out*
> *murderous threats against the Lord's disciples.*
> *He went to the high priest and asked him for*
> *letters to the synagogues in Damascus, so that*
> *if he found any there who belonged to the Way,*
> *whether men or women, he might take them as*
> *prisoners to Jerusalem. As he neared Damascus*
> *on his journey, suddenly a light from heaven*
> *flashed around him. He fell to the ground and*
> *heard a voice say to him, "Saul, Saul, why do*
> *you persecute me?" "Who are you, Lord?" Saul*
> *asked. "I am Jesus, whom you are persecuting,"*
> *he replied (Acts 9:1-5 NIV).*

Paul was astonished to learn the truth. He had blindly, wholeheartedly believed that those who followed Jesus were endangering the Jewish law and religious traditions. Besides, he knew Jesus had been crucified, so he thought they must be stopped from perpetuating "lies" about His resurrection. But now, He couldn't deny that Jesus was alive. He had heard and seen Him.

Interestingly, the religious leaders had also been deceived. They had previously agreed with Paul, and they also wanted to stop the disciples from spreading what they thought were fabrications about Christ. Some of them even suggested that the disciples should be killed, but one of their leaders tried to change their minds by his advice.

> Leave these men alone! Let them go! For if their purpose or activity is of human origin, it will fail. But if it is from God, you will not be able to stop these men; you will only find yourselves fighting against God" (Acts 5:38 NIV).

Here we are about two thousand years later. People are still fighting against God and feel threatened by the truth. We continue to see fervent hatred in the world today. People are so obsessed with their hatred that they can't see what is true and good. Satan's goal is to make wickedness look harmless, and worse; he wants to make what is wrong look right.

> Woe to those who call evil good, and good evil; Who put darkness for light, and light for darkness; Who put bitter for sweet, and sweet for bitter! Woe to those who are wise in their own eyes, And prudent in their own sight! (Isaiah 5:20-21 NKJV).

Previous to his conversion, the Apostle Paul was raised in a religious environment. He knew the rules well, and like all the other good Pharisees, he strictly abided by the rulebooks. By all appearances, he was probably admired and respected as a godly man. No doubt he legalistically attended all the meetings at the Synagogue and was careful to bring his offerings. Jesus had something to say to those self-righteous types.

> *Woe to you, scribes and Pharisees, hypocrites! For you pay tithe of mint and anise and cummin, and have neglected the weightier matters of the law: justice and mercy and faith. These you ought to have done, without leaving the others undone (Matthew 23:23 NKJV).*

The pharisaical attitude of legalism hurts the individuals that are caught up in it. Especially if they begin to think they are good enough by obeying the rules, instead of trusting in Jesus. This also can cause harm to the Church. In fact, before he changed and received the Grace of God, Paul's legalistic attitude wounded the Body of Christ. Jesus questioned Paul about why Paul was persecuting Him.

> *But Saul began to destroy the church. Going from house to house, he dragged off both men and women and put them in prison (Acts 8:3 NIV).*

Legalism still puts people in prison by stealing the freedom that is available through Jesus. It makes people pretend to be something they can't be. They may look good on the outside, but on the inside they're a mess. (See Matthew 23:25.) Paul was miraculously transformed from legalistic thinking. He was sleeping in deception, but God woke him up on the road to Damascus when Jesus revealed Himself.

It is always a miraculous transformation of the heart and mind when someone is converted, and no one should ever brag about how many people they have saved. God uses His children to share the Gospel, but it is only God who gives Salvation, and He deserves all the glory. And because this is true, Christians can be reassured, that everyone of us have experienced a divine, personal touch by the hand of the Lord, which brought us to faith.

> *All things have been committed to me by my Father. No one knows who the Son is except the Father, and no one knows who the Father is except the Son and those to whom the Son chooses to reveal him (Luke 10:22 NIV).*

It must have been a shocking experience for Paul to realize He had been behaving like an enemy of God, when he really thought he was doing what was right. After his Damascus Road experience, and by the power of God, Paul spread the Gospel to the Gentiles, started churches, and made missionary journeys throughout the Roman empire. He wrote more words of the Bible than any other writer, authoring 13 books of the New Testament. The following words express his humility and give us hope.

> *I'm speaking to you out of deep gratitude for all that God has given me, and especially as I have responsibilities in relation to you. Living then, as every one of you does, in pure grace, it's important that you not misinterpret yourselves as people who are bringing this goodness to God. No, God brings it all to you. The only accurate way to understand ourselves is by what God is and by what he does for us, not by what we are and what we do for him (Romans 12:3 MSG).*

Although Paul had been deceived, he received the truth when God presented it, because he was teachable. Everyone has been exposed to deception in one form or another. If we are open to the truth and seek it in humility, even if that means we have to swallow our pride because we were wrong in our thinking, we will be set free.

> So if the Son makes you free, you will be free indeed (John 8:36 NASB).

We can hardly escape deception while we live in this world. To mention a few places, we see it in politics, the media, schools, leadership, organizations, and with our associations. There are no areas on this planet where the devil hasn't attempted to take control and bring in his diabolical plans. He's continually trying to turn people from the truth by his trickery.

> But evil men and impostors will grow worse and worse, deceiving and being deceived (2 Timothy 3:13 NKJV).

To keep ourselves from being deceived, we can be strengthened by the Word of God and learn the facts to keep ourselves pure and free. Although the devil will surely come to us and try to make us listen to him and accept his lies, we don't have to allow him to stick around.

In a memorable analogy, O.S. Hawkins compared our minds to a hotel where anyone can enter the lobby. "The manager cannot keep someone from entering the lobby; however, he can certainly keep that person from getting a room." [16] Similarly, we can manage our hearts and minds and keep the enemy from dwelling there.

> So let God work his will in you. Yell a loud no to the Devil and watch him scamper. Say a quiet yes to God and he'll be there in no time. Quit

> *dabbling in sin. Purify your inner life. Quit*
> *playing the field (James 4:7-10 MSG).*

We need to be aware of demonic permeation, anywhere we go in this world. Maybe, like me, you have felt it particularly strong in certain places. One example is, sometimes when I'm shopping at the mall, I can feel the satanic presence of the spirit of greed beckoning me as I look at certain expensive, luxurious merchandise – and if I don't get out of that environment quick, I would probably spend my money foolishly.

> *Why spend money on what is not bread, and*
> *your labor on what does not satisfy? Listen, listen*
> *to me, and eat what is good, and you will delight*
> *in the richest of fare (Isaiah 55:2 NIV).*

It isn't that we can't have and enjoy opulent things, but there are usually better ways to use our money. Plato said, "Everything that deceives may be said to enchant."[17] In previous chapters, I contrasted the importance of plainness and simplicity, compared to worldly thrills, showing that the human appetite for tantalizing nonessentials can be a dangerous thing.

> *A prudent person sees trouble coming and ducks;*
> *a simpleton walks in blindly and is clobbered*
> *(Proverbs 27:12 MSG).*

Another area where caution is needed is in the entertainment industry. There is a cunning, satanic thrust, which brings powerful deception through what is shown on the screen. The depiction of sinfulness is so common, that some have forgotten what sin is, and what it can do. So, the following are a few reminders of how immorality, no matter how small the impurity to which we may carelessly permit, can deceive and bring great trouble.

Sin makes us blind; sin brings poor judgement; sin brings disaster; sin steals peace; sin destroys love; sin confuses; sin causes illness; sin has punishment; sin is costly; sin destroys our testimony. I could go on, but you get the point.

> *You were taught, with regard to your former way of life, to **put off** your old self, which is being corrupted by its deceitful desires (Ephesians 4:22 NIV).*

Holiness and purity are an uncomfortable subject to some people. Maybe that's why we don't hear it preached very much. I've even felt some discomfort in sharing what sin can do, partly because it seems so preachy, but it's probably because I'm preaching to myself too. Nevertheless, the truth should never be diluted. I truly believe our need for deliverance from deception is a matter of urgency - for the whole world.

> *If we claim to be without sin, we deceive ourselves and the truth is not in us. If we confess our sins, he is faithful and just and will forgive us our sins and purify us from all unrighteousness (1 John 1:8-9 NIV).*

VISION CHECK FOR CHAPTER 7

1. Before his conversion, the Apostle Paul tried to silence Christians, and he thought he was doing what was right. Has God corrected a wrong belief that you had about something, and if so, briefly explain.

2. Read Matthew 23:25-28, and tell what you think the outside of the cup and the inside of the cup are referring to in this passage. Also, what will make the cup clean?

3. What harm can a gossip do? (See Proverbs 16:28)

4. Is it possible to keep ourselves from error without Jesus? (See John 15:5).

5. According to Matthew 7:15, what do false prophets look like?

6. Read Matthew 10:16. How should Christians behave among predators?

7. According to 1 John 4:20, what is a characteristic of a liar?

8

LigHt

Then Jesus again spoke to them, saying, "I am the Light of the world; he who follows Me will not walk in the darkness, but will have the Light of life" (John 8:12 NASB)

Last week, I enjoyed the sunshine as I sat outside reading. When I heard the phone ring, I got up quickly and rushed inside my house to answer it. After being in the bright sunlight, my eyes hadn't adjusted to my comparatively dark living room, and I ran full force into an end table, tripped, fell and injured my leg. This wouldn't have happened if I had just flipped on the light switch, easily available by the door. But alas, today I'm limping around with a leg that's still sore because I didn't take the time to do that.

The world we live in is full of a different kind of darkness with an unseen enemy waiting to trip those who have no light. However, the Light is easily available to those who want to walk in it.

> *For You have delivered my soul from death, Indeed my feet from stumbling, So that I may walk before God In the light of the living (Psalm 56:13 NASB).*

God has given us a resource which can literally give us sight, physically and spiritually. Since you're reading this book, I'm pretty sure you have this resource in your possession (and if you don't, it's pretty easy to get it). It can give us faith, hope, peace, confidence, wisdom and knowledge to mention a few wonderful things. Within its pages we can find the keys to health, prosperity and safety. Furthermore, it shows us the future and teaches about things invisible – things that we could never figure out on our own.

> *Ask me and I will tell you remarkable secrets you do not know about things to come (Jeremiah 33:3 NLT).*

Most importantly, the Word of God gives us life because it is the Bread of Life. Is there any other book or anything else in the world that can offer that? It's surprising how many people pursue an education and yet never study the Bible. What good are all the educational institutions and many forms of learning if one never sees the truth about life?

> *Always learning and never able to come to the knowledge of the truth (2 Timothy 3:7 NKJV).*

Nothing else contains the powerful, life applicable truths for us like the Bible. I'm repeating myself for emphasis, but the Bible and our great need for it is an inexhaustible subject. I can't help but be excited about it because the Word is powerfully alive. Something incredible happens when the scriptures are heard, read or spoken. It is guaranteed to accomplish something good.

> So shall My word be that goes forth from My mouth; It shall not return to Me void, But it shall accomplish what I please, And it shall prosper in the thing for which I sent it (Isaiah 55:11 NKJV).

The Bible is a treasury of wisdom, knowledge and great promises; yet, it often gathers dust, unused, on our coffee tables and in bookcases. Although this health-conscious generation may be conscientious about eating nutritional meals and carefully considering what they put in their mouths, many of those same people are neglecting their spiritual needs and becoming terribly undernourished.

> Jesus answered, "It is written: 'Man shall not live on bread alone, but on every word that comes from the mouth of God'" (Matthew 4:4 NIV).

There are places in the world where the Bible is not readily available, and where it is even prohibited. There are demonic enemies of the truth that want to destroy the Bible, the Church and our liberty. In America, we are very fortunate that we still have rather easy accessibility to the Word of God. This is a precious freedom for which we take for granted. But it's becoming more obvious that not everyone likes what is true and right.

There are those who hate the one who upholds justice in court and detest the one who tells the truth (Amos 5:10 NIV).

Unfortunately, many people, including so-called Christians, don't take advantage of our privileged freedom. Although the scriptures will illuminate our way and keep us from calamities so we won't stumble and fall, without knowing what it says and applying the truth to our lives, we will certainly falter in the dark. (See Psalm 140:4-5.) The late Rev. Billy Graham said, "It's not enough to turn from the darkness. To live in the light and punch holes in the darkness, you must plug in to God."[18] Then we can have peace.

You will not fear the terror of night, nor the arrow that flies by day, nor the pestilence that stalks in the darkness, nor the plague that destroys at midday. A thousand may fall at your side, ten thousand at your right hand, but it will not come near you (Psalm 91:5-7 NIV).

We hear a lot of excuses for not reading the Bible. Here are a few: "**I don't like to read**." Almighty God has chosen to speak to you personally this way, so surely it would be worth working at it, even if you don't like to read. "**I'm not a good reader**." Then listen to a recording of the Word, or start with an easy-to-read translation, or even a children's Bible. "**I don't retain what I read**." We may have to read a passage repeatedly before we digest it, but digging for treasure takes a little time. (See Psalm 119:73.) And lastly, please don't use the common excuse, "**I'm too busy**." Nothing you can possibly be doing is more important hearing from the Lord.

> *Take my yoke upon you. Let me teach you,*
> *because I am humble and gentle at heart, and*
> *you will find rest for your souls. For my yoke is*
> *easy to bear, and the burden I give you is light*
> *(Matthew 11:29-30 NLT).*

Men who were inspired by God wrote the Bible, but God Himself is the author. The Bible contains the very words of God, which can have no private interpretation (see 2 Peter 1:20), and it will define itself. There are counterfeit renderings and readings erroneously shared in cults and false religions which are presented as truth from God, but the true Church rejects them as heresies. (See Galatians 1:8 and John 10:27.)

The only way we can grasp the meaning of the words in the Bible is through the light of the Holy Spirit, and there is so much that He can show us. Reading the Bible is an underestimated, immeasurable, profitable endeavor. If we could actually see the invisible, divine power that is manifested to us through studying the Word, I think we'd work at it a lot more.

> *All Scripture is inspired by God and is useful*
> *to teach us what is true and to make us realize*
> *what is wrong in our lives. It corrects us when*
> *we are wrong and teaches us to do what is right.*
> *God uses it to prepare and equip his people to do*
> *every good work (2 Timothy 3:16-17 NLT).*

Neglecting to take time to study the Bible for any reason is a decision to walk in darkness. We need the Word for survival. Every day we make a choice whether or not to "turn on the light" or leave ourselves vulnerable to "falling."

When I sit by myself and read the Word, it's like spending quality time with my best friend. Relationships don't develop unless we give our time to get to know them. (See John 17:3.) So, if you haven't ever read the Bible through at least once, make that your goal. Even if you only take a few minutes to read it each day, it can do more for your life than all the hours you spend doing other things. As you are diligent in studying and reading it, you can expect it will whet your appetite for more. (See Matthew 5:6.) We want more when we taste something really good.

> Oh, taste and see that the LORD is good; Blessed is the man who trusts in Him! (Psalm 34:8 NKJV).

For those of us who have tasted, it seems unimaginable that there are those who won't make the choice to taste all that Jesus offers. Many remain in the bland life that they've chosen (see 2 Corinthians 2:15-16), and they have no appetite for righteousness. But there is a reason for their choice.

> Everyone who does evil hates the light, and will not come into the light for fear that their deeds will be exposed. But whoever lives by the truth comes into the light, so that it may be seen plainly that what they have done has been done in the sight of God (John 3:20:21 NIV).

God's Light brings conviction, and also repentance, which is mandatory for forgiveness. (See Luke 13:2-5.) Maybe you've heard the term, "Easy Believism," which has been described as a theology that teaches that all you have to do is believe in Jesus, and all your sins are quickly washed away. The fact is, there are those who believe "there is a God," but they aren't saved, because their pride holds them back and they haven't repented.

> *You believe that there is one God. You do well.*
> *Even the demons believe--and tremble! (James*
> *2:19 NKJV).*

The serious business of repentance is found throughout the Bible. Jesus preached the need for repentance from the time He began to preach. (See Matthew 4:17.) In Acts 2:38, we see that Peter advised us that we should repent and be baptized for the forgiveness of our sins, and in Revelation 3:3, we are again warned to repent.

The Light of God will continue to bring His children to humility and repentance, and the recognition of our personal sin isn't just a onetime experience when we receive Jesus as Savior. Throughout our lives, the Holy Spirit will help us to identify and convict us of sin. (See John 16:8.) But remember, the light of conviction is different than the dark feeling of condemnation, which actually comes from the devil.

> *This is the message which we have heard from*
> *Him and declare to you, that God is light and*
> *in Him is no darkness at all (1 John 1:5 NKJV).*

While He walked on the earth, Jesus said He was the Light of the world (see John 9:5); however, He transferred that Light to His disciples to carry on with the Gospel because He ascended into Heaven. Today, those of us who are followers of Christ are also given this responsibility of continuing to share the truth. The Light of God was placed within us when we were born again.

> *For God, who said, "Let light shine out of*
> *darkness," made his light shine in our hearts to*
> *give us the light of the knowledge of God's glory*

displayed in the face of Christ (2 Corinthians 4:6 NIV).

God has placed His hope in us, and He is calling for us to shine for Him and pass on the Light. He has entrusted His imperfect, mistake-making, fragile, children with the duty to share His message, so that other blind and lost people can be saved too. And we can do it because He has empowered us. (See Luke 10:18-19.) Until that day when we are fully rescued from darkness, let us grow and share His marvelous Light.

And there will no longer be any night; and they will not have need of the light of a lamp nor the light of the sun, because the Lord God will illumine them; and they will reign forever and ever (Revelation 22:5 NASB).

VISION CHECK FOR CHAPTER 8

1. What did Jesus promise us in John 8:12, and what does Psalm 146:8 say that God gives?

2. List two of the benefits of walking in the Light as found in 1 John 1:7.

3. Psalm 119:105 NIV says, *Your word is a lamp to my feet, a light to my path.* Explain briefly what that means to you in one sentence.

4. Read Revelation 3:3 and tell why there is danger in delaying to repent.

5. What alternative ways or resources can you suggest for studying the Bible?

6. What did Jesus pray for the Father to do for His followers in John 17:17?

7. What specific advice can be applied to your life from 2 Timothy 2:15?

9

Anticipation

*My soul, wait silently for God alone, For my
expectation is from Him (Psalm 62:5 NKJV).*

Looking at scrumptious pictures in a restaurant menu
can make our mouths water before we even taste the food,
because we expect it to be delicious. We don't doubt that the
electric skillet will get hot when we plug it in, the icemaker
will dump ice as we hold a glass under it, and the sun will
set in the evening and rise in the morning. We depend on
our alarm clocks to buzz when it's time to get up in the
morning, our phone calls to go through to the right number,
the mail to be delivered, the water heater to heat and so on
and so on.

You've probably guessed that I'm trying to make a point.
And my point is, we anticipate the action or the result of a
lot of stuff, which are comparatively trivial things. Dare I say

that many of us Christians probably have more assurance that water will pour from a faucet when we turn it on, than we have for expecting God to move in our lives?

Actress, Helen Mirren was quoted as saying, "What gift do you think a good servant has that separates them from the others? It's the gift of anticipation."[19] I think she was probably talking about an attribute she found in a good maid or butler; however, I was thinking what she said is also applicable to a servant of Christ.

> We keep looking to the LORD our God for his mercy, just as servants keep their eyes on their master, as a slave girl watches her mistress for the slightest signal (Psalm 123:2 NLT).

Most of us don't use our minds enough for anticipating that Jesus Christ could show up at any second. If we did, it would be more obvious by what we are doing with our daily lives.

In Exodus 12:1-11, we learn that the Lord told Moses and Aaron how the Israelites should make themselves ready for their rescue from slavery and their exodus from Egypt, along with preparing and eating the Passover lamb.

> This is how you are to eat it: with your cloak tucked into your belt, your sandals on your feet and your staff in your hand. Eat it in haste; it is the LORD's Passover (Exodus 12:11 NIV).

I find that verse to be a good reminder that we should keep ourselves ready to go at all times. In the same way that the Israelites were ready to go as they waited for their exodus out of Egypt, we also wait for our liberation. And actually, it's not just our ultimate departure to which I'm referring.

It is also a continuing anticipation of our daily rescue. Like them, we too should feel expectant for God's deliverance.

> In the morning, LORD, you hear my voice; in the morning I lay my requests before you and wait expectantly (Psalm 5:3 NIV).

The influence of the world on our lifestyles, and its many distractions, keep our thought lives too cluttered with small and insignificant matters, but God wants us to mature and begin to think differently. It isn't that he wants us to be oblivious to worldly considerations, but rather to keep our spiritual life and our relationship with Him in the forefront. We can refocus.

When my husband and I are on a road trip, and we need to see what's ahead on the highway, we can use our binoculars to see what's further up the road so we can be prepared. In our various everyday matters, we never know what we'll encounter on the road of life, but God will always prepare us for what is ahead as we look to Him. The Bible teaches us how to be ready, in season and out of season, always watching for God.

> You are my strength, I watch for you; you, God, are my fortress (Psalm 59:9 NIV).

The things that preoccupy our minds are a measure of our spiritual maturity. For example, we are told to pray continually, "*without ceasing.*" (See I Thessalonians 5:17 NKJV.) Bible teacher, O.S. Hawkins wisely explains what he believes that means: "We should live our lives in a constant state of communion with God as we go about our work and witness."[20] Perhaps that sounds idealistic and impossible, but

God will never ask us to do something impossible...without His help. Through Him, we can do the impossible - even in our thought life. (See Matthew 17:20.)

> *People with their minds set on you, you keep completely whole, Steady on their feet, because they keep at it and don't quit (Isaiah 26:3 MSG).*

One of the keys in good advertising is that in order to successfully sell a product to the public, a positive and exciting anticipation must somehow be created in the consumer. Boring advertisements don't stimulate the imagination, nor do they encourage people to make a purchase. The customer must be influenced in such a way that the product looks appealing and stirs his appetite. An informative article, about the power of anticipation in advertising and its influence, explains that "anticipation precedes all action" and "impacts consumer decisions." [21] We can relate that explanation to a mindset of anticipating God to move in our lives: Anticipating the Lord causes us to act, and it impacts our decisions. That is encouraging and there is nothing boring about that.

The enthusiasm that we have as Christians, and our genuine anticipation of God's promises to us, can generate hope. People are starved for it, and hope and positivity are contagious to those around us. Imagine what could be generated if all the believers in church on Sunday morning came together anticipating God to do something special. Instead of expecting the service to be the same old thing, there would be a refreshing sense of excitement and waiting on the Lord.

> *I would have despaired unless I had believed that I would see the goodness of the LORD In the*

> *land of the living. Wait for the LORD; Be strong*
> *and let your heart take courage; Yes, wait for the*
> *LORD (Psalm 27:13-14 NASB).*

Despair will develop in people who are negative or who don't expect good things, but positive expectations produce joy. Definitions of anticipation include "realization in advance; foretaste, expectation or hope."[22] We will certainly be watching closely if we anticipate something good is forthcoming. Even though there will always be distractions, we can do our best to concentrate more on what matters the most.

> *It will be good for those servants whose master*
> *finds them watching when he comes. Truly I tell*
> *you, he will dress himself to serve, will have them*
> *recline at the table and will come and wait on*
> *them. It will be good for those servants whose*
> *master finds them ready, even if he comes in*
> *the middle of the night or toward daybreak. But*
> *understand this: If the owner of the house had*
> *known at what hour the thief was coming, he*
> *would not have let his house be broken into (Luke*
> *12:37-39 NIV).*

Keeping ourselves ready for the unforeseen is important. To mention several things in our culture, most of us pay for all kinds of insurance in preparation for unexpected accidents. We buy generators, batteries, candles and matches to have on hand in case the electricity goes off during bad weather. Furthermore, some of us are a bit notorious for keeping a large over-supply of toilet paper. We want to be prepared. Besides, nobody likes the embarrassment of unpreparedness. I've had enough moments like that in my life.

I remember the mortification I felt the day I tried on some beautiful shoes I found at a fancy clothing store. I didn't expect to be buying new shoes on that shopping trip, but when I saw them in the store window, I couldn't pass them up. Unfortunately, I forgot I was wearing an ugly pair of socks with a big hole in them, and the handsome clerk who was helping me couldn't hold back his snicker. My face turned beet red. I don't want to be embarrassed and unprepared like that again. But being ready is especially necessary in our spiritual life.

> *So you also must be ready, because the Son of Man will come at an hour when you do not expect him (Matthew 24:44 NIV).*

Throughout the Bible, you see the people of God, ready and expecting God to move. David anticipated slaying the giant, Goliath, with only a simple slingshot in his hand. Noah anticipated the waters to subside after the flood. The centurion anticipated that Jesus would heal his servant. The Virgin Mary anticipated giving birth to the Son of God.

> *And Mary said: "My soul glorifies the Lord and my spirit rejoices in God my Savior, for he has been mindful of the humble state of his servant. From now on all generations will call me Blessed, for the Mighty One has done great things for me— holy is his name. His mercy extends to those who fear him, from generation to generation (Luke 1:46-50 NIV).*

We see Mary's strong faith and hope in those joyful words. Our hearts, through words, also reveal what we anticipate. (See Luke 6:45.) Everyone has some kinds of expectations, whether good or bad. For example, we tend to expect people to behave a particular way, we expect our workday will go a certain way, and we have assumptions in our mind about whether things will be enjoyable, beneficial or successful …or not.

> *The desire of the righteous is only good, But the expectation of the wicked is wrath (Proverbs 11:23 NKJV).*

In the end, we pretty much get what we expect. Expectation begins every day, as soon as we get out of bed in the morning. The late Norman Vincent Peale taught that the mind always tries to complete what it pictures. If we make it a point to picture positive outcomes in every situation, especially when we feel threatened or intimidated, we will more likely see positive results. On the other hand, the enemy wants to try to catch us off guard with negativity, and he will try to make us entertain his dreadful conjectures of disastrous consequences.

> *Keep a cool head. Stay alert. The Devil is poised to pounce, and would like nothing better than to catch you napping (1 Peter 5:8 MSG).*

Beginning the day with prayer and Bible reading is a preventative to the wiles of the enemy. Also, if used properly, using our imaginations to picture something good can be a very helpful tool for keeping us positive and cheerful. Again, we can do this by replacing those bad mental pictures, which the devil will attempt to make us dwell on, and anticipating what is good. This task of the renewing of the mind, mentioned in Romans 12:2, needs to be a regular endeavor in order to keep ourselves from chaos.

> *You will keep in perfect peace all who trust in you, all whose thoughts are fixed on you! (Isaiah 26:3 NLT).*

The Apostle Paul advised that we should always be anticipating the coming of Christ. That state of mind will surely make a difference in our attitudes each day. Anticipation is a powerful scriptural principle. Believers can look forward to what is coming because they know that God is always working. (See John 5:17).

> *I wait for the LORD, my whole being waits, and in his word I put my hope (Psalm 130:5 NIV).*

VISION CHECK FOR CHAPTER 9

1. Read Psalm 27:14, then tell of one situation where this instruction can be applied to your personal life.

2. What would be the opposite instructions to the wise advice in Psalm 37:7?

3. What good thing can Christians anticipate, as found in Romans 8:22-23

4. Name two things on which you can meditate, as suggested in Philippians 4:8-9?

5. Think of a negative thought you've had. Then think of how you could replace that thought by anticipating something good. Write that positive replacement for future thinking in the space below.

6. Hope is expectation that something good is going to happen. Picture a positive answer to a prayer request, and describe how your prayer might be answered.

7. Why do you think it is important to be anticipating Jesus' return?

10

Picturing God

For since the world began, no ear has heard, and
no eye has seen a God like you, who works for
those who wait for him! (Isaiah 64:4 NLT).

Do you have some kind of picture of God in your mind? Do you see God in shiny robes, feathery wings and a golden halo? Probably not. Perhaps you picture Him sitting on a huge majestic throne. Or maybe you see Jesus still hanging on the cross in His horrible suffering. Can you imagine Him coming in the clouds with His mighty hand stretched out toward you? I suppose some of us have been influenced by paintings of what someone thinks He looks like.

I love the memorable story of the young child who showed his teacher the picture he was drawing, proudly announcing that it was a picture of God. The teacher informed the boy that no one could know what God looks like. Unwavering, the child responded, "They will when I get done." [23]

To mention more famous artists, over the centuries Leonardo da Vinci, Raphael, El Greco, Rubens, Salvador Dali, Michelangelo and Diego Velazquez among others, have attempted to picture Christ in their extraordinary artwork. In awe, we may gaze at their artistic renderings and wonder, "Can this be Jesus?"

I personally like the touching illustrations by the talented, Frances Hook, and especially the one with the title, "Jesus And The Little Children." But what does God really look like? Despite all the beautiful paintings and creative interpretations which supposedly represent the Lord, none can give the complete description that the Bible gives.

> *In the beginning was the Word, and the Word was with God, and the Word was God (John 1:1 NKJV).*

The fundamental belief of Christianity is that Christ is God Himself, clothed in human flesh. Hebrews 1:3 tells us that Jesus is the exact representation of God. And the Bible gives us "pictures" of what Jesus looks like. We learn that Jesus was fully human when He dwelled on earth, but we aren't given a lot about his physical description.

> *For He grew up before Him like a tender shoot, And like a root out of parched ground; He has no stately form or majesty That we should look upon Him, Nor appearance that we should be attracted to Him. (Isaiah 53:2 NASB).*

In His humanity, Like us, Jesus had a body, soul and spirit, but scripture elaborates most on his soul and spirit.

His soul includes his mind (see Romans 15:5), will (see Matthew 26:42) and emotion (see John 11:35). And the Lord's spirit is mentioned in the book of Luke before Jesus died.

> *And when Jesus had cried out with a loud voice, He said, "Father, 'into Your hands I commit My spirit.' " Having said this, He breathed His last (Luke 23:46 NKJV).*

Beginning with the book of Genesis, all of Scripture points to the Lord and brings spiritual descriptions of Him. Again and again, the picture we have of God is the Lord Jesus Christ.

> *Yet for us there is one God, the Father, of whom are all things, and we for Him; and one Lord Jesus Christ, through whom are all things, and through whom we live (1 Corinthians 8:6 NKJV).*

In the fourteenth chapter of John, Thomas and Philip also seemed to be very interested in seeing what God looked like. Jesus had indicated that He would be going to His Father soon, and they wanted to get a more distinct picture of what He was talking about. Jesus answered them with words I'm sure they never forgot.

> *"If you had known Me, you would have known My Father also; and from now on you know Him and have seen Him." Philip said to Him, "Lord, show us the Father, and it is sufficient for us." Jesus said to him, "Have I been with you so long, and yet you have not known Me, Philip? He who has seen Me has seen the Father; so how can you say, 'Show us the Father'? Do you not believe that*

I am in the Father, and the Father in Me? The words that I speak to you I do not speak on My own authority; but the Father who dwells in Me does the works (John 14:7-10 NKJV).

Faith is always necessary for anyone to get a clearer picture of God. Since we get faith by hearing the Word, I might extend the expression, "A picture is worth a thousand words" by adding "...but the Word of God gives us the greatest picture." However, we learn that those who don't have faith, won't see the picture.

And He said: 'I will hide My face from them, I will see what their end will be, For they are a perverse generation, Children in whom is no faith (Deuteronomy 32:20 NKJV).

On the other hand, God befriends and reveals Himself to those who have faith and keep his commandments. The Message version of John 14:21 indicates that God will make Himself plain to those who know and obey Him.

No one has ever seen God, but the one and only Son, who is himself God and is in closest relationship with the Father, has made him known (John 1:18 NIV).

The Bible tells us about the people who have had incredible visions of the Lord. For instance, Ezekiel described what he saw:

Like the appearance of a rainbow in the clouds on a rainy day, so was the radiance around him. This was the appearance of the likeness

CONNie BerteLSeN YouNg

> of the glory of the LORD. When I saw it, I fell
> facedown, and I heard the voice of one speaking
> (Ezekiel 1:28 NIV).

In the book of Revelation, John tells of the glorious vision he had seeing Christ:

> Then I turned to see the voice that spoke with
> me. And having turned I saw seven golden
> lampstands, and in the midst of the seven
> lampstands One like the Son of Man, clothed
> with a garment down to the feet and girded about
> the chest with a golden band. His head and hair
> were white like wool, as white as snow, and His
> eyes like a flame of fire; His feet were like fine
> brass, as if refined in a furnace, and His voice as
> the sound of many waters; He had in His right
> hand seven stars, out of His mouth went a sharp
> two-edged sword, and His countenance was like
> the sun shining in its strength (Revelation 1:12-
> 16 NKJV).

In Bible times, there were other people who had visions from God. including Jacob, Samuel, Daniel, Nathan, Isaiah, Obadiah, Amos, Zechariah, Peter, Ananias and Paul, to mention a few. After Jesus rose from the dead He appeared to his disciples, but that was not a vision.

> Later on that day, the disciples had gathered
> together, but, fearful of the Jews, had locked
> all the doors in the house. Jesus entered, stood
> among them, and said, "Peace to you." Then he
> showed them his hands and side. The disciples,
> seeing the Master with their own eyes, were
> exuberant (John 20:19-20 MSG).

Thomas was not there on that day when Jesus appeared to the disciples, and he let them know there was no way he could believe without touching the scars in Jesus' hands and side. When Jesus came through the locked doors and appeared to the disciples again, he spoke very personally to Thomas.

> *Then he said to Thomas, "Put your finger here, and look at my hands. Put your hand into the wound in my side. Don't be faithless any longer. Believe!" "My Lord and my God!" Thomas exclaimed. Then Jesus told him, "You believe because you have seen me. Blessed are those who believe without seeing me" (John 20:27-29 NLT).*

Although no one has seen God, the Father, at any time (see 1 John 4:12), He promises to live in us as we love each other. Every bit of genuine love, which we've ever personally given or received from anyone throughout our entire life, originated with God. God is love! And love gives us a picture of God like no other.

Also, another way to picture God is to look at yourself. Of course, you won't see his face and body in the mirror; nevertheless, we know He made humans like Himself.

> *This is the written account of the descendants of Adam. When God created human beings, he made them to be like himself. He created them male and female, and he blessed them and called them "human" (Genesis 5:1-2 NLT).*

Those people who don't believe in eternal life are badly deceived to think that the physical body is the essence of one's life. God originally created mankind to be spirit beings.

When Adam and Eve sinned, their spirit life died, just as God said they would die. And because all humans inherited that spiritual death, it's necessary for us to be born again so that we may really live – and really live forever!

> *Flesh gives birth to flesh, but the Spirit gives birth to spirit. You should not be surprised at my saying, 'You must be born again (John 3:6-7 NIV).*

After we have received Jesus as our Savior, God Himself is born within us through the Holy Spirit, and we become the representatives of God. I might say, a picture of God.

> *God made him who had no sin to be sin for us, so that in him we might become the righteousness of God (2 Corinthians 5:21 NIV).*

Imagine that. You can be the righteousness of God. (See 1 John 4:13-16.) He has done the work to make us right so people can see a picture of God through you. As children of God, we can all be His spokespersons and emissaries.

> *Therefore, we are ambassadors for Christ, as though God were making an appeal through us; we beg you on behalf of Christ, be reconciled to God (2 Corinthians 5:20 NASB).*

That's our responsibility as Christians. And although we haven't seen exactly what the Lord looks like, we've known His love. We can make His love visible by the way we live. Then finally, someday soon, every eye will see Him in all His glory.

Dear friends, we are already God's children, but he has not yet shown us what we will be like when Christ appears. But we do know that we will be like him, for we will see him as he really is (1 John 3:2 NLT).

❧❦

VISION CHECK FOR CHAPTER 10

1. Read 1 Timothy 1:17 and list 2 (or more) characteristics of God.

2. What similarities do we share with Christ in his humanity in the way we are made?

3. See John 20:29 and fill in the blank: Those who have never seen Jesus but believe in Him will be _____.

4. Where does John 1:1 say that Jesus was in the beginning (before He was born of the Virgin Mary in Bethlehem)?

5. Have you ever received a vision, and if so, share what you saw.

6. Describe what you think God looks like with as few words as possible.

7. According to Habakkuk 2:14, what will fill the earth?

11

Lies

But the cowardly, unbelieving, abominable, murderers, sexually immoral, sorcerers, idolaters, and all liars shall have their part in the lake which burns with fire and brimstone, which is the second death (Revelation 21:8 NKJV).

Author, Israelmore Ayivor wrote, "Some words are sweet but unprofitable! Some are bitter but important. First weigh your words on the counter of integrity and speak not only because your words are sweet, but because they contain the truth!"[24]

Not only should we carefully weigh our words before we speak, we must evaluate the words we hear. Jesus warned about the falsities that would certainly be prevalent in the end times.

Then if anyone says to you, 'Look, here is the Christ!' or 'There!' do not believe it. For false christs and false prophets will rise and show

> *great signs and wonders to deceive, if possible,*
> *even the elect. See, I have told you beforehand*
> *(Matthew 24:23-25 NKJV).*

Knowing his time is short (see Revelation 12:12), Satan is recruiting liars, deceivers, fabricators, fakes, mockers, perjurers and betrayers. They write books, magazine and newspaper articles; they hand out flyers and knock on doors; they're news reporters, politicians and movie producers; they're in social media; they're in the school system; and they have even slipped into our churches. (See Matthew 7:15.) That's only the tip of the iceberg, or I should say more appropriately, a mere spark of hellfire.

> *Not a word from their mouth can be trusted;*
> *their heart is filled with malice. Their throat is*
> *an open grave; with their tongues they tell lies.*
> *Declare them guilty, O God! Let their intrigues*
> *be their downfall. Banish them for their many*
> *sins, for they have rebelled against you. But let*
> *all who take refuge in you be glad; let them ever*
> *sing for joy. Spread your protection over them,*
> *that those who love your name may rejoice in you*
> *(Psalm 5:9-11 NIV).*

Oliver Wendell Holmes said, "Sin has many tools, but a lie is a handle that fits them all."[25] Lies can cloud our lives, erode our relationships, affect our health and hurt our faith. I apologize for this negative view; however, we are indeed being bombarded with evil, and we must not be unmoved, but instead watch with awareness, defend our faith and share the truth.

> *Keep your eyes open, hold tight to your*
> *convictions, give it all you've got, be resolute,*

CONNIe BerteLSeN YouNg

and love without stopping (1 Corinthians 16:13-14 MSG).

The world in which we live has become increasingly sinful - but you probably already know that without being told it again. We think of the righteous saints that have passed on before us, and we've said something like, "If they could see us now…they would be horrified!"

If the foundations are destroyed, What can the righteous do? (Psalm 11:3 NKJV).

That question is essentially this: If the world is collapsing because it is out of order in diabolic leadership, compromising laws and sinful behaviors, and if Biblical principles are disregarded and despised, then what can Christians do? What is our part?

Let love be without hypocrisy. Abhor what is evil; cling to what is good (Romans 12:9 NASB).

We can pray. "Lead us not into temptation, but deliver us from evil." Meanwhile, we must not become desensitized to that which is indeed evil. Since this world is so full of disregard for the Bible's instruction in righteousness, people can become dangerously insensitive and blind to what is sinful. For instance, what we view on our television is not all harmless, but how quick we can be enticed by something on the screen which eventually becomes immoral, perverted or misleading.

Do not be deceived: "Evil company corrupts good habits" (1 Corinthians 15:33 NKJV).

Sometimes the television brings evil company into our homes. Meanwhile, it is erroneous to think that the more we grow in our Christian faith, the less we will need to resist evil. Think about it. You may not want to hear this, but faithfulness will bring out the wicked. If you are committed to serving the Lord, you can be guaranteed that you'll stir up the enemy. The apostles were a good example of the right attitude in their response after hateful encounters.

> *The apostles left the high council rejoicing that*
> *God had counted them worthy to suffer disgrace*
> *for the name of Jesus (Acts 5:41 NLT).*

The very essence of ministry is to find the unsaved and bring the message of Salvation to them, so we should expect those that don't live by the truth to cross our path. And Christians will be targeted by spiritual forces of evil.

> *Submit yourselves, then, to God. Resist the devil,*
> *and he will flee from you (James 4:7 NIV).*

We can resist the devil, but don't forget the first part of that verse. Submit to God. Divine power must be activated in us through our submission to God, or our efforts are futile.

One day, Paul and Silas were interrupted as they were going to a place of prayer when a loud-mouth fortune teller started following them around.

> *She followed Paul and the rest of us, shouting,*
> *"These men are servants of the Most High God,*
> *who are telling you the way to be saved" (Acts*
> *16:17 NIV).*

Have you ever wondered how this demon-possessed, fortune teller could be talking this way? Afterall, those words were true. (Remember, even Satan quoted scripture.) Apparently, she believed there is a God – like many who believe there is a God. But that wasn't, and isn't, enough. (See James 2:19.)

God has always forbidden fortune-telling. (See Deuteronomy 18:10-12). Divination, horoscopes, witchery, sorcery, astrology and the like were in the world back in Paul and Silas' day, and they're still around in this century. It's surprising to see how many people believe lies about what is supposed to happen to them. Nevertheless, the Bible says only God knows the future.

> Since no one knows the future, who can tell someone else what is to come? (Ecclesiastes 8:7 NIV).

Obeying the truth is quite different than merely speaking the truth. That fortune teller was selective in what she chose to obey. Sadly, some who consider themselves Christians think they can pick and choose what they want to believe and apply, which is a root of hypocrisy.

> But the Spirit explicitly says that in later times some will fall away from the faith, paying attention to deceitful spirits and doctrines of demons, by means of the hypocrisy of liars seared in their own conscience as with a branding iron (1 Timothy 4:1-2 NASB).

By the power of God, Paul responded and cast out a demonic spirit from the woman who was telling lies for profit. Nowadays, also because of the love of money, deceit is widespread in our society. We see wrong stuff all the time, and I'm afraid, it doesn't always bother us much. But darkness should annoy us like it did Paul, and motivate us to respond.

> *You are the light of the world. A city set on a hill cannot be hidden; nor does anyone light a lamp and put it under a basket, but on the lampstand, and it gives light to all who are in the house (Matthew 5:14-15 NASB).*

Because of the lies that were perpetuated against Paul and Silas and their ministry (see Acts 16:19-22), the crowd turned against them instead of standing with the truth. The devil has always used false propaganda.

Aldous Huxley wrote, "The greatest triumphs of propaganda have been accomplished, not by doing something, but by refraining from doing." [26] Voices through the news, politicians, social media, the opinions of our acquaintances, family, etc., could cause us to be swayed, biased or silent about what we believe. Weighing the validity of someone's views with the Bible will determine if they are correct or not, and this should influence our response.

> *Then you will know the truth, and the truth will set you free (John 8:32 NIV).*

Indeed, the truth will set us free, but that doesn't mean we won't suffer. Paul and Silas were insulted, beaten and thrown in prison; yet, they began singing praises to God. (See Acts 16:23-25.) Nevertheless, A lot was accomplished by their faith and obedience. Later, they were miraculously rescued, and the jailer and his whole household were saved.

No enemy, no lies, or hardships will ever be able to keep

the Church from being built. Jesus told Peter that it would be built despite our dreaded opposition.

> And I also say to you that you are Peter, and on this rock I will build My church, and the gates of Hades shall not prevail against it (Matthew 16:18 NKJV).

Here we are in the twenty-first century, and the Church is still very much alive. One would think that the evidence of that fact alone should dispel the lies of heretics; nevertheless, the truth continues to be rejected and distorted.

> But even if we, or an angel from heaven, preach any other gospel to you than what we have preached to you, let him be accursed (Galatians 1:8 NKJV).

Apostates and counterfeit churches are always around, but we can identify them by authoritative, Biblical criterion. The Bible reveals the crux of true and false religion, and certain predominant beliefs can be recognized in both.

I'll mention three examples that are symptomatic of heresy:

- Those who attest that Jesus isn't God and He was only a man
- Those that believe that having enough good works is what will earn your way to Heaven
- Those that think the Blood of Christ has little or no significance

Also, when looking closely, we may find that within false religions and cults there is frequently a spirit of superiority, self-righteousness, prejudice, legalism, and the keeping of dogmata and various beliefs contradictory to scripture.

> *For the time will come when they will not endure sound doctrine; but wanting to have their ears tickled, they will accumulate for themselves teachers in accordance to their own desires, and will turn away their ears from the truth and will turn aside to myths (2 Timothy 4:3-4 NASB).*

The epitome of true religion is love and faith in Jesus Christ, and complete reliance on His payment by His Blood for our sins. And the Word of God is <u>always</u> the final answer.

> *I rejoice in your word like one who discovers a great treasure. I hate and abhor all falsehood, but I love your instructions (Psalm 119:162-163 NLT).*

VISION CHECK FOR CHAPTER 11

1. List two things depictive of pure religion that are noted in James 1:27.

2. Read Ezekiel 12:2, and tell what you think makes people unable to see the truth?

3. What is something that characterizes an imposter? (See Jude 1:12-13.)

4. From where is our struggle against darkness originating, as indicated in Ephesians 6: 11-12?

5. According to Romans 12:21, how should you overcome evil? Give an example.

6. The truth may hurt, but the Bible shows us that lies are what really hurt us. What happens to liars according to Proverbs 19:5?

7. Can you think of something that might sway people away from what is true and right?

12

Mystery

Just as you cannot understand the path of the wind or the mystery of a tiny baby growing in its mother's womb, so you cannot understand the activity of God, who does all things (Ecclesiastes 11:5 NLT).

There's a remarkable story in the Old Testament about Daniel and how he responded to Nebuchadnezzar, who audaciously demanded that someone should interpret his strange dream. (See Daniel 2:26-48.) Daniel bravely indicated to the king that it was impossible for any human to reveal mysteries, but then he reassured him that God could reveal mysteries.

Daniel's exceptional life clearly showed that, for him to have the ability to understand anything, he depended completely on his faith in God. Some seemingly, implausible events distinguished his life because of his uncommon faith.

As it turned out in that particular story, God miraculously gave Daniel a detailed interpretation of Nebuchadnezzar's dream. The king was so taken with his explanation, that he promoted Daniel to a high position, and gave him many gifts. I hope you'll be encouraged in knowing, today, there remains *a God in Heaven who reveals mysteries.*

There was a monumental mystery that was hidden for centuries, which is most significant to our lives. That mystery was revealed through the birth of Jesus Christ, Savior of the world.

> *Then the angel said to them, "Do not be afraid, for behold, I bring you good tidings of great joy which will be to all people. For there is born to you this day in the city of David a Savior, who is Christ the Lord (Luke 2:10-11 NKJV).*

We hear those scriptural words about that stupendous mystery, especially repeated in December, when we celebrate Christmas. As we look at the angel's words closely, we see they contain applicable information for every month and day of our lives. The momentous birth and life of Christ continues to reveal mysteries for all people who receive Him.

> *Now to Him who is able to establish you according to my gospel and the preaching of Jesus Christ, according to the revelation of the mystery which has been kept secret for long ages past, but now is manifested, and by the Scriptures of the prophets, according to the commandment of the eternal God, has been made known to all the nations, leading to obedience of faith; to the only wise God, through Jesus Christ, be the glory forever. Amen. (Romans 16:25-27 NASB).*

In the last chapter, I wrote about the darkness which comes from people and evil spirits who lie; however, we need not be deceived by lies because we have the light of God's Word. We know that the light of truth is so much more powerful than the darkness of wickedness, regardless of its extent.

> *The light shines in the darkness, and the darkness can never extinguish it (John 1:5 NLT).*

I like what Craig Stone said, "Lies are ants, the truth is the sun, and questions are a magnifying glass waiting to be picked up by the curious."[27] This quote inspired me to use a picture of a magnifying glass for this chapter. It represents a tool for which we can look at things closely. Then, whatever we want to see will be expanded so it can be seen clearly.

> *Indeed, if you call out for insight and cry aloud for understanding, and if you look for it as for silver and search for it as for hidden treasure, then you will understand the fear of the LORD and find the knowledge of God. For the LORD gives wisdom; from his mouth come knowledge and understanding (Proverbs 2:3-6 NIV)*

The Word of God contains great wisdom with answers to parables and mysteries that may not be seen easily. As our eyes and hearts look closely at the words therein, the Holy Spirit brings magnification and gives us understanding.

I remember the first time I determined to read the Bible. Frankly, it was like trying to speedily walk through heavy, deep water. Despite my early enthusiasm for gaining quick understanding of the Bible, I was forced to move slowly, plugging along. Eventually, some truths became clearer as I persevered and sincerely searched for the Lord with all my heart. Yet, there is always more to learn.

> *Make me understand the way of Your precepts,*
> *So I will meditate on Your wonders (Psalm 119:27 NASB).*

Albert Einstein said, "One cannot help but be in awe when he contemplates the mysteries of eternity, of life, of the marvelous structure of reality. It is enough if one tries merely to comprehend a little of this mystery every day. Never lose a holy curiosity." [28]

Jesus spoke mysteries in parables. One day He explained to the disciples the reason He did that. (I like the Message Bible version of what was implied; however, you might take the time to look at other Biblical translations of Mark 4:10-11 for a more complete perspective.)

> *When they were off by themselves, those who were close to him, along with the Twelve, asked about the stories. He told them, "You've been given insight into God's kingdom—you know how it works. But to those who can't see it yet, everything comes in stories, creating readiness, nudging them toward receptive insight (Mark 4:10-11 MSG).*

It seems that at times, Jesus purposely gave a limited view, using parables. Nevertheless, He knew that hearing even a glimpse of the truth would always whet the appetite of those who truly want to know the truth. Yet unfortunately, sometimes, illumination of the bare facts brings discomfort, and even hostility to some individuals.

> And the judgment is based on this fact: God's light came into the world, but people loved the darkness more than the light, for their actions were evil. All who do evil hate the light and refuse to go near it for fear their sins will be exposed. But those who do what is right come to the light so others can see that they are doing what God wants (John 3:19-21 NLT).

We all sin (see Romans 3:23), and it's uncomfortable to see our badness, but Jesus indicated that He wants to rescue us from sin, not condemn us. Rescue will happen when we are willing to fully submit ourselves to Him and admit our sin. Then, for us who receive Him, we trade our sin for His righteousness. (See Romans 3:22.) This is a mystery that some fail to see.

> But we speak God's wisdom in a mystery, the hidden wisdom, which God predestined before the ages to our glory; the wisdom which none of the rulers of this age has understood; for if they had understood it, they would not have crucified the Lord of glory (1 Corinthians 2:7-8 NASB).

I believe Salvation is the greatest mystery ever to be discovered by anyone. There are still many people who haven't received this amazing free gift. I've always thought that generally, Christians are too unaware of how concealed the mystery of Salvation is to unbelievers. We tend to forget that we were also blind until the Lord mercifully brought us to the Light, and we might assume that anyone should easily grasp it. But it is truly a gift given only given by God. Rather than being smug in the wonderous, privilege of Salvation, it should humble us that He chose to give it to us. Praise Him!

> *For You are my lamp, O LORD; And the LORD*
> *illumines my darkness (2 Samuel 22:29 NASB).*

Again, the power to grasp the truth and comprehend the facts in the Word of God always comes through the Holy Spirit. (See 1 Corinthians 2:14.) We are promised that wisdom is given to those who ask for it. Let's ask for wisdom today.

> *But if any of you lacks wisdom, let him ask of*
> *God, who gives to all generously and without*
> *reproach, and it will be given to him (James 1:5*
> *NASB).*

Most of us would like the reputation of being a wise and knowledgeable person. We want to have the smarts to handle everything well, whether it be from things like preparing our income tax, making wise investments or purchases, using our time well, dealing with relationships, or just having the brains to make good choices as we live in this world. Wisdom will surely help us in all those things, but the ultimate purpose of wisdom is to know God.

> *I keep asking that the God of our Lord Jesus*
> *Christ, the glorious Father, may give you the*
> *Spirit of wisdom and revelation, so that you may*
> *know him better (Ephesians 1:17 NIV).*

In case you don't know it yet (although I think you do), the best resource of wisdom and revelation so that you may know God, is the Bible. The Word intensifies our relationship to the Lord, establishes our faith, strengthens our heart and mind, exposes our enemy and instructs us so we may grasp those mysteries which were once imperceptible to us.

Within the Bible, we find many examples of mysteries revealed to the people of God. Here are a few examples: In Luke 1:34-35, the Virgin Mary was told how the Son of God would be conceived. The mystery of what will happen to the faithful after death is explained in I Corinthians 15:51-54. In 1 Timothy 3:16, we learn that Christ is the mystery of Godliness. And in the following words, Paul wrote about the mystery of Jews and Gentiles sharing the promise in Christ in the following words to the Ephesians.

> *None of our ancestors understood this. Only in our time has it been made clear by God's Spirit through his holy apostles and prophets of this new order. The mystery is that people who have never heard of God and those who have heard of him all their lives (what I've been calling outsiders and insiders) stand on the same ground before God. They get the same offer, same help, same promises in Christ Jesus. The Message is accessible and welcoming to everyone, across the board (Ephesians 3:5-6 MSG).*

The Jewish ancestry before Paul didn't understand everything that was prophesized to them in their day, but like us, they were required to live by faith, believing that what God promised would surely come about someday. (See Habakkuk 2:3-4.) There continues to be mysteries for which we have yet to receive answers. Meanwhile, while we live by faith, we only *"see in a mirror, dimly."* (See 1 Corinthians 13:12 NKJV.)

> *Oh, the depth of the riches both of the wisdom and knowledge of God! How unsearchable are His judgments and His ways past finding out! (Romans 11:33 NKJV).*

VISION CHECK FOR CHAPTER 12

1. Read Psalm 111:10. What is the basis for getting understanding and wisdom?

2. Is there a mystery or a question pertaining to your personal life for which you have (or have not) prayed for answers?

3. According to 1 Corinthians 13:2, what is more important than understanding mysteries?

4. Can you always see the reason that God allows certain things to happen to you? (Read Ecclesiastes 11:5 and 2 Corinthians 5:7.)

5. What mystery or plan has God made known to us in Ephesians 1:9-10?

6. What is an attribute mentioned in Romans 1:17 that we need in order to live?

7. Explain what the mystery in Colossians 1:27 means to you.

13

Revelation

Where there is no revelation, people cast off restraint; but blessed is the one who heeds wisdom's instruction (Proverbs 29:18 NIV).

Dictionary definitions of the word "revelation" include "an act of revealing or communicating divine truth" and "something that is revealed by God to humans."[29] And like the Bible verse says, without it, people *case off restraint* - which means, without revelation, we don't obey God.

Some people think that God no longer gives us revelation today, but take another look at the above verse. Obviously, if we need revelation in order to remain obedient to God, we can be certain that He would continue to provide it. Besides, God is the same yesterday, today and forever.

> *"For I am the LORD, I do not change; Therefore*
> *you are not consumed, O sons of Jacob (Malachi*
> *3:5 NKJV).*

Surely, God continues to bring revelation to those He loves. The following verse is one example, and I believe that the most significant revelation ever given to mankind can be found in this verse.

> *For God so loved the world that He gave His*
> *only begotten Son, that whoever believes in Him*
> *should not perish but have everlasting life (John*
> *3:16 NKJV).*

That verse expresses the epitome of Christianity, and it is probably one of the most well-known verses in the Bible. This joyous promise is for everyone who will receive it. Yet, the message contained there needs to be embraced and personalized, or it remains mere words without application. Sadly, there are many who don't get it.

> *Enter by the narrow gate; for wide is the gate*
> *and broad is the way that leads to destruction,*
> *and there are many who go in by it (Matthew*
> *7:13 NKJV).*

Jesus denounced the people who refused to repent and apply the truth, even after he showed them numerous miracles. (See Matthew 11:20-21.) Apparently, revelation is hidden from such people, while God gives it to others - and interestingly, the ones who get it are not the individuals that one would ordinarily assume to be recipients of that precious knowledge. Jesus seemed to be rather happy about that fact. And I am too.

> At that time Jesus said, "I praise You, Father,
> Lord of heaven and earth, that You have hidden
> these things from the wise and intelligent and
> have revealed them to infants (Matthew 11:25
> NASB).

In a portion of the same passage the Message Bible reads, "*You've concealed your ways from sophisticates and know-it-alls, but spelled them out clearly to ordinary people.*"

It appears that a humble person is more likely to receive divine revelation, so we should try our best to be humble. Humility is characterized in a modest view of self, a lack of arrogance, and a quiet trust in the wisdom of God. But we don't see humility in people who are always preoccupied with themselves. In fact, self- assertion based in pride will block revelation. Pride is like a blindfold that hides the wisdom of God.

> And even if our gospel is veiled, it is veiled to
> those who are perishing. The god of this age has
> blinded the minds of unbelievers, so that they
> cannot see the light of the gospel that displays
> the glory of Christ, who is the image of God (2
> Corinthians 4:3-4 NIV).

There are invaluable advantages which are given to us as children of God, and humility and child-likeness, opens up the Kingdom treasury. Because the Spirit of God lives within us, we are given access to what is good and true.

> In Him we have redemption through His blood,
> the forgiveness of sins, according to the riches
> of His grace which He made to abound toward
> us in all wisdom and prudence, having made

> known to us the mystery of His will, according to
> His good pleasure which He purposed in Himself
> (Ephesians 1:7-9 NKJV).

God speaks to us and gives revelation in various ways. Of course, He will speak to us through the Bible, but He is not limited in the way He discloses the truth we need for our lives. For instance, He often speaks through people or personal experiences. In fact, He's most likely trying to speak to you through whatever is happening to you right now. Think about the current circumstances in your life. There may be an important message within those things you're experiencing. You can believe He always has something to say to each of us, but we must be listening and waiting to hear from Him.

> I will hear what God the LORD will speak, For
> He will speak peace To His people and to His
> saints; But let them not turn back to folly (Psalm
> 85:8 NKJV).

A wise person said, "Often times, we pray to God with expectations around the kinds of answers we want to receive back, instead of just listening to what God is telling us through our situations and circumstances."[30] Until we realize that God's answers for us are so much better than anything we think we require, or that we can decide, we will keep rolling around in disappointment, doubt and self-pity. Instead, we can abide in the joy of trusting His perfect judgements. (See Nehemiah 8:10 and 2 Corinthians 12:9.)

> For as the heavens are higher than the earth, So
> are My ways higher than your ways, And My
> thoughts than your thoughts (Isaiah 55:9 NKJV).

We receive revelation as we absorb verses such as that one. This is an essential truth that must be embraced for a victorious life, because if it isn't believed, there will continue to be hesitation in settling the matter of dying to self and fully trusting His judgements instead of our own.

> *For we know that our old self was crucified with him so that the body ruled by sin might be done away with, that we should no longer be slaves to sin (Romans 6:6 NIV).*

While there remains any belief that our ways and thoughts are superior, we are not completely submitted to the Lord, and we will miss His perfect plan. Perhaps the concept of revelation is made too glamorous for some. The fact is, we don't have to be brilliant theologians to personally receive revelation from the Holy Spirit. Furthermore, I think I'm correct in saying that anyone who has not absolutely received revelation from the Lord, is not a true Christian.

While you're still gasping at that bold thought, think about this: W. Tozer wrote, "For it is not mere words that nourish the soul, but God Himself, and unless and until the hearers find God in personal experience, they are not better for having heard the truth."[31] Paul said something regarding the necessity of hearing from God to the followers of Christ in his day. (See Hebrews 5:12-14.) He also related his personal experience with which Christians can identify.

> *I did not receive it from any man, nor was I taught it; rather, I received it by revelation from Jesus Christ (Galatians 1:12 NIV).*

The question many of us have is, "How do I get more of this precious revelation from the Lord?" O.S. Hawkins wrote, "Since being unresponsive, unperceptive, unteachable and unrighteous is the condition in our natural state, something outside of us must intervene to enable us to become responsive to the gospel, perceptive of the things of God, teachable, and righteous before Him."[32] Then Hawkins prudently concludes according to Philippians 1:6, that Christ began the work in us, and He will finish it!

Indeed, it is God who brings more revelation, but it isn't automatic just because we say we are Christians. King David gave his son, Solomon, some very good advice which we can apply to our own lives.

> As for you, my son Solomon, know the God of your father, and serve Him with a whole heart and a willing mind; for the LORD searches all hearts, and understands every intent of the thoughts. If you seek Him, He will let you find Him; but if you forsake Him, He will reject you forever (1 Chronicles 28:9 NASB).

The chosen people of God, and that includes you if you've made Jesus Christ your Lord, have been called out of darkness. (See 1 Peter 2:9.) Not only the darkness of our foolish thinking, but also out of worldliness. The wicked ways of the world seem to ooze darkness every way we turn, but as we submit to the Lord, He gives us the marvelous light of revelation and guides our every step.

> Your ears shall hear a word behind you, saying, "This is the way, walk in it," Whenever you turn to the right hand Or whenever you turn to the left (Isaiah 30:21 NKJV).

The eleventh chapter of the book of Hebrews reminds us of a basic requirement for anyone to have illumination from God. We learn about Noah, Abraham, Moses and others who possessed faith. They experienced meaningful, unclouded direction for their lives, because of their faith. They believed God, and received divine information and personalized attention from the Lord.

> But without faith it is impossible to please Him,
> for he who comes to God must believe that He is,
> and that He is a rewarder of those who diligently
> seek Him (Hebrews 11:6 NKJV).

Those ancients realized that God rewards those who "*diligently seek Him.*" In order for us to find revelation, we have to be intently looking for it.

I've used the term "Kingdom treasure" which includes unlimited revelation, wisdom, knowledge, and the power of Almighty God. Don't wait until Heaven to see it, because it's available in the here and now. But I know, we all have a tendency to take it for granted. Too often we wait until there is a crisis, and then we plead for the information or the help that we need. Jesus indicated that if we don't continually abide in Him, we'll dry up and get burned.

> If anyone does not abide in Me, he is thrown
> away as a branch and dries up; and they gather
> them, and cast them into the fire and they are
> burned. If you abide in Me, and My words abide
> in you, ask whatever you wish, and it will be
> done for you (John 15:6-7 NASB).

Don't wait until you have an emergency or until you're already in that fire. (See Isaiah 55:6.) We are way too fragile and vulnerable when disconnected from the Lord, but every resource of strength, truth and revelation is available, as we remain in Jesus.

Perhaps you have within your heart a burning desire to receive revelation from God. Then receive the Psalmist's advice:

> *Delight yourself also in the LORD, And He shall give you the desires of your heart (Psalm 37:4 NKJV).*

VISION CHECK FOR CHAPTER 13

1. Read Luke 2:29-32. To what was Simeon referring to as he thanked God for *a light for revelation*?

2. Name something that may cause blindness as suggested in 2 Corinthians 4:4.

3. Has God given you personal revelation, and if so, what was it?

4. According to the Psalmist, what sort of people does God guide and help? (See Psalm 25:8-9.)

5. Jesus said we need to become like little children (Matthew 18:3), so how would you describe the qualities of child-likeness that influences your ability to get revelation?

6. What could be a reason we haven't received an answer that we want according to James 4:2?

7. Is there a specific question in your mind for which you want a divine answer?

14

Stupefying Vastness

That He would grant you, according to the riches of His glory, to be strengthened with might through His Spirit in the inner man, that Christ may dwell in your hearts through faith; that you, being rooted and grounded in love, may be able to comprehend with all the saints what is the width and length and depth and height-- to know the love of Christ which passes knowledge; that you may be filled with all the fullness of God (Ephesians 3:16-19 NKJV).

One of my favorite places to visit is Glacier Point in Yosemite National Park. The massive, panoramic sights of the incredible peaks of Yosemite's high country, Half Dome, Yosemite Falls and all the fantastic, sweeping views from that high place are positively breathtaking. When looking down from the tip of the Point, I see the glorious Yosemite

Valley, 2,700 feet below, making my heart beat a little faster as I peer down that grand drop to the distant valley.

When I behold this wondrous view, I can't help but pause to remember, God formed these mountains and prepared this exquisite view – still, nothing compares to His magnificence.

> *You are glorious and more majestic than the everlasting mountains (Psalm 76:4 NLT).*

The massive beauty of what can be seen from Glacier Point is truly spectacular. The many wonders of the world are remarkable, and the universe in all its splendor is staggering, but contrasted to the awesome, incomparableness of God, who existed before the world was created, those things are nothing. (See Psalm 90:2.) Although we may try to express who God is with our thoughts and words, they are inadequate, and we will always fail to give a worthy description of His vastness.

> *Thine, O LORD, is the greatness and the power and the glory and the victory and the majesty, indeed everything that is in the heavens and the earth; Thine is the dominion, O LORD, and Thou dost exalt Thyself as head over all. Both riches and honor come from Thee, and Thou dost rule over all, and in Thy hand is power and might; and it lies in Thy hand to make great, and to strengthen everyone (1 Chronicles 29:11-12 NASB).*

The Bible teaches us that no one has seen God; furthermore, God is spirit, and those who worship him must worship in spirit and truth (see John 4:24.), but have you ever wished that you could have a vision or see a hint of God with your eyes? Maybe not get too close, since no one who sees Him could live - but only to be able to observe Him enough to lock the image in your memory banks for future reference, so you'd never doubt again. Then again, if we were granted that experience, I think we'd be petrified.

One day when Moses was tending the flock for his father-in-law, Jethro, the Lord appeared to Him through a burning bush. I'm, pretty sure Moses was initially terrified.

God told Moses of His plan to bring the Israelites out of Egypt and out of slavery, using Moses as their leader.

After listening to God's instructions, Moses asked God to tell him what he should tell the Israelites when they asked who sent him to be their leader. I think Moses hoped for a more precise description of God to share.

> Moses said to God, "Suppose I go to the Israelites and say to them, 'The God of your fathers has sent me to you,' and they ask me, 'What is his name?' Then what shall I tell them?" God said to Moses, "I AM WHO I AM. This is what you are to say to the Israelites: 'I AM has sent me to you'" (Exodus 2:13-14 NIV).

As I pondered why God didn't elaborate more on describing Himself, I came to the conclusion that He couldn't define Himself because a mere man simply could not comprehend it. Instead, He responded to Moses with the Hebrew words, "Ehyeh asher Ehyeh" (I AM WHO I AM) which translate as, "I will be what I will be." [33]

Putting it that way, those words indicate that God is limitless. And those "compartmentalized boxes" of various information in our human brains, can't hold it all when it comes to the immensity of God. Sometimes that makes us feel a little uncomfortable, or for some, a little out of control, which in turn, produces a feeling of fear. But that's not a bad thing.

> The fear of the LORD is the beginning of wisdom;
> A good understanding have all those who do
> His commandments. His praise endures forever
> (Psalm 111:10 NKJV).

That verse infers that we'll have a good enough understanding through our obedience. My friend, Jim Cornelius, Founder of Christian Armor Ministries wrote, "Men with no understanding do not understand that God has called them to reflect His beauty; men with no understanding do not walk in the Fear of the Lord but are led by their own human appetites. Scripture says the Fear of the Lord is to *be upon* His people, meaning it is more than something we feel, but also something we do."[34] (See 2 Chronicles 19:7.)

> Jesus replied, "Anyone who loves me will obey my teaching. My Father will love them, and we will come to them and make our home with them. Anyone who does not love me will not obey my teaching. These words you hear are not my own; they belong to the Father who sent me (John 14:23-24 NIV).

Obedience is a result of our genuine love and fear of God. For me, the fear of the Lord and the incomprehensible, immensity of God is somewhat like what I feel when standing at the peak of Glacier Point and looking thousands of feet, straight down, to the Valley below. It's beautiful...and overwhelming; and yet, the splendor of it all stirs my heart with an indescribable peace.

> *Can you search out the deep things of God? Can you find out the limits of the Almighty? (Job 11:7 NKJV).*

I don't consider the non-canonical words in the Apocrypha as Holy Scripture; however, I've considered the words that are written in Judith 8:14. "You cannot plumb the depths of the human heart, nor find out what a man is thinking; how do you expect to search out God, who made all things, and find out his mind or comprehend his thoughts?" I think that is a prudent question, nonetheless, I know that through faith, we can see what is imperceptible.

> *Now faith is confidence in what we hope for and assurance about what we do not see (Hebrews 11:1 NIV).*

I believe that God certainly wants you and I to understand what He thinks and wants for us, even though His thoughts are so much greater. And although scripture teaches us about God, we really can't understand anything about God's immeasurable self unless He shows us - and He wants to show us. For instance, the Bible shows us the hugeness of God's love. The NLT translation elaborates well.

> *And I am convinced that nothing can ever separate us from God's love. Neither death nor life, neither angels nor demons, neither our fears for today nor our worries about tomorrow—not even he powers of hell can separate us from God's*

> *love. No power in the sky above or in the earth*
> *below—indeed, nothing in all creation will ever*
> *be able to separate us from the love of God that is*
> *revealed in Christ Jesus our Lord (Romans 8:38-*
> *39 NLT).*

The Word of God reveals many other far-reaching attributes of God worth studying. To mention a few, He is a God of mercy (see Daniel 9:9), peace (see Romans 16:20), faithfulness (see Psalm 36:5), light (see 1 John 1:5) and joy (see Nehemiah 8:10). But all the many descriptions we have, still don't give us enough understanding to put in that metaphorical "compartmentalized box" that I mentioned. Nevertheless, we have been given all we need in order to receive Him.

> *But the basic reality of God is plain enough.*
> *Open your eyes and there it is! By taking a long*
> *and thoughtful look at what God has created,*
> *people have always been able to see what their*
> *eyes as such can't see: eternal power, for instance,*
> *and the mystery of his divine being. So, nobody*
> *has a good excuse (Romans 1:19-20 MSG).*

Have you ever been stirred with a glimpse of God, merely by observing His handiwork? Perhaps it was a rainbow in the sky, the sunrise after a storm, or the miracle of a newborn baby which stirred your heart to recognize Him.

> *Let us acknowledge the LORD; let us press on to*
> *acknowledge him. As surely as the sun rises, he*
> *will appear; he will come to us like the winter*
> *rains, like the spring rains that water the earth"*
> *(Hosea 6:3 NIV).*

Something special happens within our hearts as we observe and contemplate God's works and recognize God's Hand; even the mundane things in our life take on a different appearance. Simon Peter had a few, almost unimaginable experiences with Jesus in his everyday life and work. One of those times was when He and his friends had been fishing all night with nothing to show for it. But at Jesus' request, they let down their nets and caught so many fish that their nets were breaking. He was in awe over what the Lord did, and it humbled Him.

> When Simon Peter saw it, he fell down at Jesus' knees, saying, "Depart from me, for I am a sinful man, O Lord!" (Luke 5:8 NKJV).

Peter's saw the boundless capability of the Lord and he was surely enthralled, but his appreciation and recognition of what he saw God do was not the end of his response. He fully committed his life to Christ.

In Matthew 19:27 NKJV, Peter told Jesus, "*We have left everything to follow you.*" Can we say we have "left everything" to follow the Lord? Sometimes, unlike Peter, our attitude of reverence only remains while we see and feel God move. Then, when the momentary inspiration is gone, we tend to go back to our old ways. It makes me think that some of those religious, miracle event gatherings are overrated; that is, if worship is diminished unless the power of God is obviously displayed.

J.B. Phillips wrote, "We have not only to be impressed by the size and unlimited power of God, we have to be moved to genuine admiration, respect, and affection if we are ever to worship Him."[35]

Now to him who is able to do immeasurably more than all we ask or imagine, according to his power that is at work within us, to him be glory in the church and in Christ Jesus throughout all generations, for ever and ever! Amen (Ephesians 3:20-21 NIV).

VISION CHECK FOR CHAPTER 14

1. (See Ephesians 3:16-19.) Paul wrote to the Ephesians indicating that he wanted them to be able to *comprehend* the love of Christ; yet, he also said *the love of Christ passes knowledge.* Why isn't this a contradiction?

2. In Isaiah 55:9, we learn that God's thoughts are much greater than ours, so how can we know any of God's thoughts? (See 1 Corinthians 2:10-12.)

3. According to Proverbs 2:5, what great benefit is associated with the fear of God?

4. Which person of the Godhead was Paul referring to in 1 Timothy 6:16 that no one has ever seen?

5. Is it possible that the Bible contains every single thing that God has ever done? (See John 21:25.)

6. According to Hebrews 11:1, how can we find assurance and evidence about God?

7. Is there a place in the world where you have visited, or a particular experience that you've had, that reminded you of the vastness of God?

15

SiMPLiCiTY

*Stand fast therefore in the liberty by which Christ
has made us free, and do not be entangled again
with a yoke of bondage (Galatians 5:1 NKJV).*

After writing the last chapter, Stupefying Vastness, it seemed
appropriate for me to consider the "other end of the tunnel,"
which is somewhat easier to define. Besides, this is a sweet
subject to me. I really like simplicity.

To mention a few things, I prefer things such as simple
menus and meals, plain clothing and jewelry, inconspicuous
decor and designs, and easy to operate tools and devices. I
find a single, rosebud more beautiful than a whole garden
of flowers. I don't care for complicated security systems,
appliances with unnecessary control knobs and switches, or
technology that seems to require rocket scientist mentality

in order to understand it. Furthermore, I desire things like smooth running relationships, well-planned vacations, and straightforward business meetings. To me, simplicity is a synonym for peace. And since I'm a firm believer in, "The more the words, the less the meaning" (see Ecclesiastes 6:11 NKJV), that's all I'm going to say about my personal choices.

Simplicity of heart is seen in the lives of the early Christians. They devoted themselves to the apostles' teaching, and a joyful simplicity was a main element in their lives.

> *So continuing daily with one accord in the temple, and breaking bread from house to house, they ate their food with gladness and simplicity of heart praising God and having favor with all the people. And the Lord added to the church daily those who were being saved (Acts 2:46-47 NKJV).*

It is a fallacious belief to think that living in simplicity means that one will be deprived. Instead, it's really only a matter of keeping basic, important things as priorities. The real deprivation is when our thoughts and hearts are cluttered and confused with insignificant considerations that keep us from enjoying God's purpose for us.

Hoarding is an extreme example of a sickness that happens to people who have lost tract of keeping the right priorities. They become so fixated on gathering and holding material things tightly, that they are unable to see what really matters. I suppose we all have some tendency to do that in different degrees. If you don't believe me, ask yourself if there is anything that you own that you would hate to give away.

> *"I have the right to do anything," you say—but not everything is beneficial. "I have the right*

*to do anything"—but I will not be mastered by
anything (1 Corinthians 6:12 NIV).*

Dejan Stojanovic wisely said, "The most complicated skill is to be simple."[36] I'm sure you realize that in this rat race world of hustle-bustle, restlessness and strife, simplicity is not easy to find. Maybe you can identify with the words in the following Psalm. It was written when David longed to find a peaceful place and escape the troubles that surrounded him.

*Oh, that I had wings like a dove; then I would fly
away and rest! I would fly far away to the quiet
of the wilderness (Psalm 55:6-7 NLT).*

It's easy to see that not everyone in the world likes quiet and simplicity. In fact, some individuals seem to thrive on surrounding themselves with continuous commotion and busyness. Those types are often found in crowds, noisy public places, or in their involvement with lots of activities and organizations. It is their choice, because not everyone prefers a quiet lifestyle.

I like what Tolstoy wrote in War and Peace. "Truth is ever to be found in the simplicity, and not in the multiplicity and confusion of things." [37] I admire people who can handle many things in a balanced way, but I wonder if we can really be fulfilled when we're pursuing labyrinthine, action-packed lives.

*Better is a dry morsel and quietness with it Than
a house full of feasting with strife (Proverbs 17:1
NASB).*

I can remember turning on the radio, only because my home seemed unnervingly quiet after being around a lot of people, and when finding myself all alone. But when being alone is bothersome, it is indication that I've forgotten that God is always with me.

> *The LORD is with me; he is my helper. I look in triumph on my enemies. It is better to take refuge in the LORD than to trust in humans (Psalm 118:7-8 NIV).*

Some households never-ever turn off their televisions. But we may need to be careful that we don't turn to noise and busyness in an attempt to cope with life through a kind of escapism. Although it may be done unconsciously, this is a way which some choose to avoid their problems which they resist addressing. With all their coming and going, their vehicles are rarely parked in their garages. They don't want to be still. (See Psalm 46:10.) But if we try to drown out our problems instead of confronting them, they will only continue to surface.

> *For God is not the author of confusion but of peace, as in all the churches of the saints (1 Corinthians 14:33 NKJV.)*

It is wise to stop and take a close look at ourselves now and then, to do a little inventory and determine if our lives have become unnecessarily chaotic. We can ask ourselves, "Am I experiencing a lot of confusion?" "Do I have peace about how I'm using my time?" "Am I doing anything I want, or am I doing what God wants?"

> *There is a way which seems right to a man, But its end is the way of death (Proverbs 14:12 NASB).*

God's way for us is much more simplified and fulfilling than the muddled path we make for ourselves when we don't follow His direction. But the devil wants to blur our focus by messing with our priorities. He tries to convince us that we know what we're doing on our own. Then if he can get us overly busy and involved in doing our own thing (which incidentally, he probably suggested), and complicate us with things that don't have any value, we're in big trouble. Frankly, I know this from my own experience.

I know Satan relentlessly attempts to distract us and keep us from using our time wisely. You better believe that, because if he succeeds in doing it, you'll lose your reward, feel dissatisfied, and look back on your life with horrible regret.

> *You have had enough in the past of the evil things that godless people enjoy—their immorality and lust, their feasting and drunkenness and wild parties, and their terrible worship of idols (1 Peter 4:3 NLT).*

Depressed people are usually those individuals who haven't experienced the fulfillment of God's plan in their lives. (See Jeremiah 29:11.) They may be deceived to think that they have no purpose - but that's because they have only pursued their own way without believing the truth. We've all been like that at one time or another. The words of Jesus give us hope.

> *"Come to Me, all who are weary and heavy-laden, and I will give you rest. "Take My yoke upon you, and learn from Me, for I am gentle and humble in heart; and YOU SHALL FIND*

> REST FOR YOUR SOULS. "For My yoke is
> easy, and My load is light." (Matthew 11:28-30
> NASB)

Hasn't everyone been "weary and heavy-laden" at one time or another? I don't know about you, but it's not unusual for me to feel that way by the end of a busy week – but it might be any day of the week when dealing with stress. So how do we get and maintain that easy yoke and light load that Jesus promises?

We need refreshment. I find it interesting to see the Biblical answer instructing us how we can be refreshed. It didn't used to be my first thought when I needed relief, but I've learned, this is the answer:

> Repent therefore and be converted, that your sins
> may be blotted out, so that times of refreshing
> may come from the presence of the Lord (Acts
> 3:19 NKJV).

Repentance is tremendously important to refreshment, and I think that the conversion advised in that verse begins with our minds. Even if our hearts have already been converted to Christianity, our thinking can still get us into a pit of despair when our focus gets off track. This happens when we begin to concentrate on the negatives instead of using our faith to halt the artillery aimed at us.

> above all, taking the shield of faith with which
> you will be able to quench all the fiery darts of
> the wicked one (Ephesians 6:16 NKJV).

When we need renewal, faith, along with repentance is very significant to our revival. We find it easy when at last we surrender, and then we wonder why it took us so long to do something so simple to get strengthened. The following Psalm is a beautiful example showing David's experience in surrendering all his troubles and expressing his faith.

> *I love you, LORD; you are my strength. The LORD is my rock, my fortress, and my savior; my God is my rock, in whom I find protection. He is my shield, the power that saves me, and my place of safety. I called on the LORD, who is worthy of praise, and he saved me from my enemies (Psalm 18:1-3 NLT).*

It may seem like a contradiction for me to say that keeping simplicity in one's life is a battle, since battles can be quite complicated. But, if indeed our defense is in place, and our priorities are established, it won't be that difficult.

> *Test yourselves to make sure you are solid in the faith. Don't drift along taking everything for granted. Give yourselves regular checkups. You need firsthand evidence, not mere hearsay, that Jesus Christ is in you. Test it out. If you fail the test, do something about it (2 Corinthians 13:5 MSG).*

In the movie, "The Alamo," John Wayne, who played Davy Crockett, epitomizes simplicity in speaking the line, "There's right and there's wrong. Y'gotta do one or the other. You do the one and you're living. Do the other and you may be walking around, but you're dead as a beaver hat."[38]

God's Way for our lives is really pretty plain and basic. Jesus made it crystal clear in His responses to those who were looking for the bare facts for living an unadulterated life.

> Jesus replied: "'Love the Lord your God with all your heart and with all your soul and with all your mind.' This is the first and greatest commandment. And the second is like it: 'Love your neighbor as yourself.' All the Law and the Prophets hang on these two commandments" (Matthew 22:37-40 NIV).

VISION CHECK FOR CHAPTER 15

1. In Matthew 6:33, what did Jesus recommend for us to do which will surely keep our lives from becoming too frazzled with wrong priorities?

2. When do you think pursuing worldly gratification or self-indulgence has gone too far? (See Titus 2:12-14.)

3. We may feel dissatisfied and bored with simple things now and then, but what does 1 Timothy 6:8 advise?

4. Can you identify one complication in your life that may be keeping you from perfect peace? (See Isaiah 26:3.)

5. On a scale of 1-5, rate the simplicity of your life this past week (with 1 indicating you were perfectly contented and peaceful, and 5 being too complicated and overwhelming).

6. When things in life become burdensome to us, what does Psalm 55:22 advise?

7. According to Philippians 4:11-13, what was the source of Paul's contentment?

16

Inescapable Conclusion

> *"Look, he is coming with the clouds," and "every eye will see him, even those who pierced him"; and all peoples on earth "will mourn because of him." So shall it be! Amen (Revelation 1:7 NIV).*

Whether or not you believe it, understand it, disbelieve it or deny it, the Lord Jesus Christ is coming again, and there will be an end to this world as we know it. No one knows exactly when He will come, but He will surely come.

> *Therefore keep watch, because you do not know on what day your Lord will come. But understand this: If the owner of the house had known at what time of night the thief was coming, he would have kept watch and would not have let his house be broken into. So you also must be ready, because*

> *the Son of Man will come at an hour when you do
> not expect him (Matthew 24:42-44 NIV).*

When I was a teenager, our family planned a road trip to Nebraska to visit relatives. I had to pack my own suitcase with clothes to take on this vacation. Although the weather was quite hot in California as we got ready to leave, little did I suspect that we'd find freezing weather and snow at our destination. The shorts and sleeveless blouses that I packed were inappropriate. I wasn't ready for the cold weather, but it was too late to go back for changes.

Although we won't be packing our suitcases with what we want to take with us when Jesus comes, we can begin readying for that day by sending something ahead. We've seen the "forecast" before we get there, and Jesus has suggested what we ought to "pack." Remember, there will be no opportunity for going back for changes.

> *"Sell your possessions and give to charity; make
> yourselves money belts which do not wear out,
> an unfailing treasure in heaven, where no thief
> comes near nor moth destroys. "For where your
> treasure is, there your heart will be also. "Be
> dressed in readiness, and keep your lamps lit. "Be
> like men who are waiting for their master when
> he returns from the wedding feast, so that they
> may immediately open the door to him when he
> comes and knocks (Luke 12:33-36 NASB).*

Keep in mind that it won't be only unbelievers who experience the consequences for not being ready. We expect the worst possible outcome for unbelievers, but even believers who don't prepare for this inevitable meeting, will experience loss. (See 1 Corinthians 3: 10-15.)

Jesus wants everyone to be ready for that day; so, He has offered His advice for how we can prepare. It would be wise for us to pay close attention to what He has said. Of course, every good thing we have comes from God in the first place, but it's obvious that He wants us to make the decision to give.

> This is how we've come to understand and experience love: Christ sacrificed his life for us. This is why we ought to live sacrificially for our fellow believers, and not just be out for ourselves (1 John 3:16 MSG).

Have you considered what things in your life would be hard for you to share or give away? You can figure if there is anything for which God asks you to surrender, it will remain your growing edge of maturity as a Christian, and the preparations which I've been writing about will remain undone, until the matter is settled between you and the Lord.

Personally, my time is an especially valuable possession for which I don't part with easily. It's usually easier to give money or things. I have to remind myself that my time belongs to the Lord, and if I'm to be submitted to Him, I should not begrudge the use of it. Choosing to use what we have for the Glory of God is a daily decision that will make an eternal difference.

> For you have been called to live in freedom, my brothers and sisters. But don't use your freedom to satisfy your sinful nature. Instead, use your freedom to serve one another in love. (Galatians 5:13 NLT).

The instructions are pretty clear, but like the rich young ruler (see Luke 18:18-23), most of us aren't too anxious to sell our precious possessions or give them away. In fact, other than a few missionaries I know, I don't know a lot Christians who have truly followed through on that for very long. Still, the following verse should inspire us.

> Give, and it will be given to you: good measure, pressed down, shaken together, and running over will be put into your bosom. For with the same measure that you use, it will be measured back to you" (Luke 6:38 NKJV).

Of course, we aren't saved by giving our stuff away, or by any of our good deeds (see Ephesians 2:8-9), but we can increase our rewards. As long as we're alive, we have occasion to "pack", so we will have treasure waiting in Heaven. This life is short, and it does seem to move faster as we get older. Hopefully, that will remind us to get busy with preparations for eternity.

> Yet you do not know what your life will be like tomorrow. You are just a vapor that appears for a little while and then vanishes away (James 4:14 NASB).

In our short lives, there are many distractions which continually interrupt our priorities. In we are advised to keep watch (see Matthew 24:42 NIV); however, Keeping watch isn't merely keeping our eyes on the clouds for Jesus' return. Keeping watch means that we must carefully guard our thoughts and heart to keep them from being polluted. We live among those who have dangerous ideas.

> You therefore, beloved, knowing this beforehand, be on your guard so that you are not carried

*away by the error of unprincipled men and fall
from your own steadfastness (2 Peter 3:17 NASB).*

In order to remove dirt from my fresh garden vegetables, I use a colander to help me as I carefully wash the vegetables before they're cooked or served. In comparison, a person's mind is like a large strainer that collects many things. Everyone is exposed to truth, lies, and various particulars that manage to find the way to our minds. It isn't that we believe everything we hear and see, or that we plan to implement all the details we collect; nevertheless, we will capture an amazing amount of data in our brains, both good and bad.

> *My dear friends, don't believe everything you
> hear. Carefully weigh and examine what people
> tell you. Not everyone who talks about God comes
> from God. There are a lot of lying preachers loose
> in the world (1 John 4:1 MSG).*

Our thoughts can be sifted, impurities identified and thrown out. A continued renewing of our minds is necessary so that we may be found clean and dressed for that upcoming marriage supper. (See Revelation 19:7.) With God's truth planted within us, we are not as vulnerable to deception. But there will always be those individuals around us who are full of error and have no intention of getting ready. They spread their doubts and want to make other people join them in their foolishness.

> *Know this first of all, that in the last days
> mockers will come with their mocking, following
> after their own lusts, and saying, "Where is the
> promise of His coming? For ever since the fathers*

> *fell asleep, all continues just as it was from the*
> *beginning of creation" (2 Peter 3:3-4 NASB).*

I've been told that I'm a fool to believe in the nonsense of the Bible. It makes me want to defend the Bible and my faith when being insulted this way, and somehow force unbelievers to see the truth. But God is my defender, and only He can save.

Biblical prophecy predicts that there will be mockers, along with a lot of other information about what will happen in the last days. Bible scholars indicate that most of the things that were predicted have already happened. In fact, it doesn't take a Bible scholar to recognize that some of those things that were prophesized many centuries ago are happening today. The following verse is one example.

> *But realize this, that in the last days difficult times*
> *will come. For men will be lovers of self, lovers of*
> *money, boastful, arrogant, revilers, disobedient*
> *to parents, ungrateful, unholy, unloving,*
> *irreconcilable, malicious gossips, without self-*
> *control, brutal, haters of good, treacherous,*
> *reckless, conceited, lovers of pleasure rather than*
> *lovers of God, holding to a form of godliness,*
> *although they have denied its power; Avoid such*
> *men as these (2 Timothy 3:1-5 NASB).*

There will certainly be an inescapable conclusion in all that God has intended for every human. I believe it will happen soon, but if it doesn't happen as soon as many Christians expect, Jesus will come in God's perfect timing. Then, no more convincing will be needed, and unbelief will vanish.

> *For it is written: "As I live, says the LORD, Every knee shall bow to Me, And every tongue shall confess to God." So, then each of us shall give account of himself to God (Romans 14:11-12 NKJV)*

Maybe you've been in a church where members of the congregation were inspired to kneel in worship. It's special to be in the presence of such reverence. But imagine all the people who were ever born, kneeling in worship together. Scientists have estimated somewhere around 100 billion people have lived on earth since the world began, although it would be impossible for them to be completely accurate in their estimates. However, whatever the number, every person who has ever lived will kneel before God.

Just like it was in the time before the flood in Noah's day, there will be many who are oblivious to their need to prepare. Things will be business as usual until Jesus returns.

> *For as in those days before the flood they were eating and drinking, marrying and giving in marriage, until the day that Noah entered the ark, and they did not understand until the flood came and took them all away; so will the coming of the Son of Man be. Then there will be two men in the field; one will be taken and one will be left. Two women will be grinding at the mill; one will be taken and one will be left (Matthew 24:38-41 NASB).*

Finally, death will be destroyed. Jesus will deliver the Kingdom to God, and darkness will be eliminated forever. (See 1 Corinthians 15:24-26.) Then at last, realities that we never dreamed about, will no longer be imperceptible!

> *The glory of the LORD shall be revealed, And all flesh shall see it together; For the mouth of the LORD has spoken"* (Isaiah 40:5 NKJV).

Even so, come, Lord Jesus!

VISION CHECK FOR CHAPTER 16

1. What did Jesus say would, and would not, pass away? (See Matthew 24:35.)

2. According to Matthew 24:14, what must happen before the end will come?

3. In 1 Timothy 4:1-3, what are two things that will be forbidden by some in later times, and who teaches these things?

CONNie BerteLSeN YouNg

4. (See Mark 13:35-37.) How can we keep watch?

5. Why should you be glad when someone insults you because of your faith in Christ? (See Matthew 5:11-12.)

6. Who will see Christ and mourn when He returns, according to Revelation 1:7?

7. What is the single word in Revelation 22:17 that the Spirit and the bride say?

AFterWord

If you confess with your mouth that Jesus is Lord and believe in your heart that God raised him from the dead, you will be saved. For it is by believing in your heart that you are made right with God, and it is by confessing with your mouth that you are saved (Romans 10:9-10 NLT).

Dear reader:

It may be that after reading this book, the Spirit of God is leading you to put your faith in Jesus Christ, and to receive the free gift of eternal life. Or perhaps, you're already a Christian and you have areas in your life that you want to fully surrender. I hope you will pray the following prayer with all your heart.

Father in Heaven: I submit myself to you. Have mercy upon me and forgive my sins. I ask You to cover me with the Blood of Jesus Christ, and change my heart and life for your Glory. Please

> *fill me with your Holy Spirit and lead me in your plan for me. I thank you for your goodness. In Jesus Name, Amen.*

If you have sincerely prayed that prayer, I believe that someday we will surely meet in Heaven!

Connie Bertelsen Young

ENdNotes

1   *The Pursuit of God* by A.W. TOZER p. 56, (Christian Publications, Inc. Harrisburg, PA, Horizon House Edition, 1976) ISBN 0-8965-010-1

2   https://www.quotemaster.org/Miracles+and+faith

3   https://www.patheos.com/blogs/christiancrier/2015/08/18/what-does-manifest-mean-a-biblical-definition-of-manifest

4   https://thewordcounter.com/what-does-dont-judge-a-book-by-its-cover-mean

5   Grace Livingston Hill *For Each New Day*, April 3RD (Barbour and Company, Inc. 1991)

6   *HEART WORDS: Considering How Words Impact Our Lives*, Westbow Press, p. 100, ISBN 978-1-9736-6654-7

7   https://en.wikipedia.org/wiki/Geraldine_Jones_(character)

8   https://www.brainyquote.com/quotes/carl_jung_142123

9   *Is God Speaking To Me?* by Lysa Terkeurst, Harvest House Publishers, p. 13 ISBN 978-0-7369-8262-7

10 https://www.lifehackorg/864437/quotes-about-setting-goals

11 https://www.healthline.com/health/how-long-does-it-take-to-form-a-habit#takeawaybecome automatic.

12 Definition of stewardship from the *Cambridge Business English Dictionary*, https://dictionary.cambridge.org/

13 *Candles In The Dark* Letters of Amy Carmichael, Christian Literature Crusade, p.4, ISBN 0-87508-085-5

14 https://addicted2success.com/quotes/50-inspirational-john-maxwell-quotes/

15 libquotes.com/stephen-covey/quote/lbm1s6r

16 *The Joshua Code*, by O.S. Hawkins, p.71, Thomas Nelson publisher ISBN-13:978-1-4003-2070-7

17 Plato, as quoted in *And I Quote*, p. 51, Applewhite, Evans & Frothingham (St Martin's Press, New York,1992).

18 https://www.billygraham.ca/stories/plugging-into-holiness

19 20+ Quotes About Anticipation - Joy - Hope (i-love-motivational-quotes.org)

20 *The Joshua Code*, by O.S. Hawkins, p.66, Thomas Nelson publisher, ISBN-13:978-1-4003-2070-7

21 www.insightsassociation.org/article/power-anticipation-and-its-influence-consumer

22 https://www.dictionary.com/browse/anticipation

23 *Chicken Soup For The Soul* written and compiled by Jack Canfield and Mark Victor Hansen, Health Communications Inc., p. 74, ISBN 1-55874-262-x

24 https://www.goodreads.com/quotes/tag/weigh

25 *Peter's Quotations* Dr. Laurence J. Peter, Bantam Books, p. 181, ISBN 0-553-27140-7

26 Aldous Huxley, *Brave New World,* foreword, As quoted in *The International Thesaurus of Quotations, P. 511,* Harper & Row, ISBN 0-06-091382-7

27 https://www.goodreads.com/quotes/1126953-lies-are-ants-the-truth-is-the-sun-and-questions

28 https://www.goodreads.com/quotes/20604-the-important-thing-is-not-to-stop-questioning-curiosity

29 https://www.merriam-webster.com/dictionary/revelation

30 https://www.beliefnet.com/faiths/christianity/6-ways-to-hear-god-more-clearly(DesireHis Voice)

31 *The Pursuit of God* by A.W. Tozer, chapter 1, p. 11, Christian Publications, Inc. Harrisburg, PA, Horizon House Edition, 1976

32 *The Joshua Code,* by O.S. Hawkins, p. 77, Thomas Nelson publisher ISBN-13:978-1-4003-2070-7

33 https://www.gotquestions.org/I-AM-WHO-I-AM-Exodus-3-14.html

34 Used by permission from Jim Cornelius, Founder of Christian Armor Ministries, www.christianarmour.net

35 *Your God Is Too Small, by* J.B. Phillips, p. 63, Macmillan Paperbacks Edition

36 https://www.goodreads.com/quotes/590771-the-most complicated skill

37 Leo Tolstoy, *War and Peace,* accessed at https.//www. goodreads.com/quotes/tag/simplicity

38 www.goodreads.com/quotes/7639612-there-s-right-and-there-s-wrong-y-gotta

Printed in the United States
by Baker & Taylor Publisher Services